Made in China

SECRETS OF CHINA'S DYNAMIC ENTREPRENEURS

Made in China

SECRETS OF CHINA'S DYNAMIC
ENTREPRENEURS

Winter Nie & Katherine Xin
with
Lily Zhang

John Wiley & Sons (Asia) Pte. Ltd.

Copyright © 2009 John Wiley & Sons (Asia) Pte. Ltd.
Published in 2009 by John Wiley & Sons (Asia) Pte. Ltd.
2 Clementi Loop, #02-01, Singapore 129809

This publication is designed to provide accurate and authoritative information
in regard to the subject matter covered. It is sold with the understanding that the
Publisher is not engaged in rendering professional services. If professional advice
or other expert assistance is required, the services of a competent professional
person should be sought.

Other Wiley Editorial Offices

John Wiley & Sons, Inc., 111 River Street, Hoboken, NJ 07030, USA
   John Wiley & Sons, Ltd., The Atrium, Southern Gate, Chichester, West Sussex
P019 8SQ, UK
John Wiley & Sons (Canada), Ltd., 5353 Dundas Street West, Suite 400, Toronto,
Ontario M9B 6H8, Canada
   John Wiley & Sons Australia Ltd., 42 McDougall Street, Milton, Queensland
4064, Australia
Wiley-VCH, Boschstrasse 12, D-69469 Weinheim, Germany

Library of Congress Cataloging-in-Publication Data
ISBN : 978-0470-82436-8

Typeset in 11/13 point, New Baskerville by Macmillan

Printed in Singapore by Saik Wah Press Pte. Ltd.
10 9 8 7 6 5 4 3 2 1

To:
Aspen and Jim
From Winter

To:
My Parents
From Katherine

To:
Yueyan and Weihna
From Lily

Contents

PART I

THE COMPETITION BETWEEN MNCs AND LOCAL POEs IN THE CHINA MARKET

CHAPTER 1

Wahaha

DANONE'S DREAM PARTNER
AND NIGHTMARE

In May 2007, Groupe Danone of France lodged a lawsuit with the Arbitration Institute of the Stockholm Chamber of Commerce, accusing Wahaha Group and three of its subsidiaries of violating the "terms of non-competition" in their joint venture deal by using the "Wahaha" brand without the approval of the joint venture. The accused three subsidiaries of Wahaha are non–joint ventures with Danone.

Since the dispute became public, the two parties have lodged a series of lawsuits. So far, as of early 2008, Wahaha has chalked up wins on legal points in China, particularly the company's hometown of Hangzhou, while Danone has claimed initial progress in legal actions outside the country. But neither side sees the dispute as winnable in a courtroom, and each has urged government officials to get involved. The fight has cut Danone's beverage business in half and is costing the company US$25 million a month in sales. And Wahaha lost leadership of the bottled-water market in China, according to Lei Yang, an ABN Amro analyst in Shanghai. In June, Tingyi, a brand from Taiwan, took the lead with a 20% share over Wahaha's 15%, Lei said, citing AC Nielsen data.[1]

The partnership seemed a good fit initially and was hailed as a model marriage. Danone brought the resources of an experienced multinational—including capital and product research—which combined well with Zong Qinghou's local knowledge. So what happened

3

to this model marriage that ended up in court? Trans-national M&As and joint ventures have always been a great challenge for multinationals' global expansion strategy. For those that plan to acquire (or set up joint ventures with) Chinese POEs (private-owned enterprises),[2] and those that compete with them in the China market, a better understanding of these local players will help the MNCs maintain a "model marriage" or gain greater competitive advantage. This is the main purpose of our book: understanding Chinese private entrepreneurs' perspectives and competing in the local turf. Let's start with the story of Wahaha and its founder Zong Qinghou.

Market Segment: The Success of a School-Run Factory

In 1979, Zong Qinghou came back to the city of Hangzhou after 15 years' farming work in the countryside in the period of the Cultural Revolution. In the following eight years, Zong managed to make a living through selling ice-creams, stationery, and textbooks for several school-run factories. In July 1987, the 42-year-old Zong registered a school-run factory (the prototype of Wahaha) with RMB 140,000 loaned capital. What they had were a less-than-20-square-meters office and three people—including Zong himself (the other two were both retired teachers). They sold textbooks and ice-creams. The profit was miserably little. For a 4 fen ice-cream, their profit was only several li.[3] Zong was determined to build up a real factory.

At that time, China's consumer products market was developing rapidly. The demand for health products was booming. Zong recalled, "There were 38 enterprises producing nutrition liquid at the time. But I found a vacancy in this market—the nutrition liquid for children." Zong had a strong sense that there existed a huge potential opportunity in this market segment. He contacted Zhejiang Medical University. Convinced by Zong's proposal, Professor Zhu Shoumin, the dean of the nutrition department, decided to develop a nutrition liquid for children.

In the summer of 1988, the nutrition liquid for children was developed. How to name this new product? Zong decided to source the name from the general public. He advertised this through the media and many people took part in the naming event. Zong chose the name Wahaha ("smiling child" in Chinese) because it's closely related to children and easily read and remembered. The design of the logo was based on the same concept—the image of a smiling child. The highly publicized event drew wide public attention for the new product. It proved to be a very successful marketing tactic, and it was free.

After that, Zong commissioned a research institute to conduct a survey among 3,000 primary school students. The survey found that 45% of the students suffered malnutrition due to fastidiousness about food, a result of Chinese parents' spoiling of their only child. At the same time as Wahaha's introduction into the market in November 1988, the result of the survey was also widely covered in the media. The commercial slogan of Wahaha was very appealing. (The voice of a child said: "Wahaha makes my food so delicious!") The first nutrition liquid for children in China thus immediately won a big market.

Wahaha sold 150,000 boxes in the first month of its launch into the market, and 200,000 boxes in the second month. Zong set up Hangzhou Wahaha Nutrition Food Factory and began the scale production of the nutrition liquid in 1989. Wahaha achieved RMB 4.88 million in sales revenue at the end of this year. In the second year, the figure reached RMB 27 million. And it soared to almost RMB 100 million in the third year.

The success of Wahaha nutrition liquid laid a solid customer base for its later product series for children (including fruit milk, calcium milk, VE calcium milk, lactobacillus milk, and fruit juice).

Purified Water: The Way to Brand Expansion

Zong was not contented with the success of the Wahaha product series for children. In early 1996, he decided to enter the purified water market. There were over 2,000 bottled-water suppliers in China at the time, 95% of them producing mineral water. As mineral water depends heavily on the water source and incurs heavy costs on transportation, it's hard to organize trans-regional sales. So there wasn't a single national brand in this market. None of the existing producers held a market share larger than 1%. Zong's judgment was that Chinese consumers were just beginning to know about bottled water. They wouldn't care about whether it's mineral water or purified water. The reverse-osmosis technology made it possible for large-scale production of purified water at low cost. Unlike the mineral water, the production of purified water didn't depend on the water source. Zong concluded that the purified water market would grow fast.

Considering the company's financial situation and the huge expenditure for promoting the new brand (an estimated RMB 100 to 200 million per year), Zong decided to extend the Wahaha brand to this new product line to leverage its brand appeal. Wahaha had been established as a brand for children, with a lively and innocent image. The target customer and brand image of purified water were quite different. It was a great challenge to make this move of brand extension. But considering there was no national brand in the purified water market, Zong was determined to take the risk. Wahaha bought seven production lines from Germany and Italy. In 1996, Wahaha purified water was launched into the market at a price 30% lower than the mineral water.

The initial advertisement of Wahaha purified water took a functional approach, attempting to make things such as the water's mineral content a selling point. Wahaha's main competitor in this market—Robust—launched its purified water at almost the same time as Wahaha. Robust's advertisement focused on "purity." Its commercial slogan was: "Robust produced purified water through 27 stages of purification." Robust won over Wahaha in the first round of advertisement campaigning. Wahaha moved quickly to show a new TV commercial. Dropping the functional theme of the old commercial, Wahaha's new commercial appealed to consumers' sentiment. The new approach made Wahaha distinguished out of the competitors. And the presence of entertainment stars enhanced its popularity. The slogan was: "You are the only one in my eye." What's more, it was broadcast on China Central Television (CCTV) and regional channels at a very high frequency. (Among all the TV advertisements for purified water at the time, an overwhelming 80% was commissioned by Wahaha.) The purified water collected a sales revenue of over RMB 500 million in 1997, which was a quarter of Wahaha's total revenue of the year. In June 1999, Hainan Yangshengtang Company (YST), the number three player of the bottled-water market, tried to use advertisement marketing to beat the number one Wahaha and the number two Robust. YST claimed in a commercial on CCTV that Nongfu Spring (the brand of YST's bottled water) was sourced from 70 meters deep in Qiandao Lake, the first-grade water source of Zhejiang. It said that other producers made purified water out of polluted water sources, and the water quality remained questionable even after purification. In July, a Beijing purified water producer sued YST for unfair competition and claimed a compensation of RMB 100,000.

In April and May of 2000, more than 20 purified water producers allied to reprimand YST. In early June, Zong also took the move to strike back at YST. Wahaha sent invitation letters to industry associations and producers of drinking water all over the country for a forum on healthy development of the industry. He called for allied efforts within the industry to protect their own interests. On June 7, delegates of the China Beverage Industry Association and 69 purified water producers attended the forum hosted by Wahaha. After the forum, the 69 producers elected their representatives to file an official charge against YST with five state supervisory organs, including SAIC[4] and MOH.[5] In July, YST sued Wahaha for circulating false information while seeking a compensation of RMB 30 million.

In June, a story was widely reported by Nanjing media. It said a local consumer found a maggot in a bottle of Nongfu Spring. The consumer lodged a suit with the local court against YST, claiming a compensation of RMB 35,000 for mental injury. YST claimed that it was being framed. In July, a consumer in Guangdong accused YST of withholding the fact of water source pollution, and claimed compensation. While the lawsuit was proceeding, another negative story against YST was made public—its registered trademark at the SAIC had not become effective. In November, YST withdrew the charges against Wahaha.

In 2000, Wahaha purified water series achieved RMB 2 billion in sales revenue with a 25% market share. Robust snatched RMB 1 billion in sales and a 15% market share. Both grew over 30%. On the other hand, Nongfu Spring achieved hardly any growth, with only a quarter of the sales of Wahaha.

Future Cola: Sharing the China Market with Pepsi and Coke

After the success of Wahaha's extension from the market for children into the market for adults, Zong decided to further expand Wahaha into the market of carbonated drinks.

Zong often said his decision was based on intuition. But this intuition was from his familiarity with the market, which was built through the first-hand information Zong gained directly from the market. Zong spent more than 200 days a year on the market frontline, visiting distributors of various tiers. He even went into the roadside shops to take a look at the products and brands on the shelf.

He paid particular attention to the serial numbers of these products, since it indicated the sales turnover—the closer the date, the better the sales. Why did one brand sell well among similar products? Was it due to its flavor, or price? How about its distribution strategy or delivery time? Zong went to the distributors for the answers to these questions. As a matter of fact, the idea of Future Cola was initiated by the first-hand information Zong gathered in this manner: it came from a suggestion made by a distributor.

The suggestion caught Zong's interest. He did some market research and found that in 1997 (the year before Future Cola was launched), carbonated drinks was only 30% of the drink products market in China. Cola drink made up just 27% of the carbonated drink products. The market potential of cola was big. As to the competitors of this market, Coke and Pepsi almost monopolized the cola market with 80% (1.36 million tons) of overall domestic output. Coke entered China in 1979; Pepsi in 1981. But it was not until 1994 that China dropped the "planned management" policy for this industry. Coke and Pepsi's rapid expansion in the China market actually started from 1994. The market penetration of Coke and Pepsi was at the first- and second-tier cities; small towns and the countryside were left vacant. According to statistics, there were over 700 million people living in the rural areas of China, which meant 70% of the total population was in the countryside and only 30% was in the urban areas including small towns.

Zong decided to use a strategy of "starting from countryside, then penetrating into cities" for his cola products. His Future Cola differentiated its target customer from Coke and Pepsi's young people in big cities by focusing on people and families of an older age in small towns and rural areas. It promoted itself as a local Chinese cola for festivities and happy family gatherings. It thus avoided a direct competition with the two soft drink giants.

It was not difficult for Wahaha's distribution network to penetrate into the market of small towns and the countryside. In its 10 years of operation, Wahaha had built up a wide distribution network. Zong called it "United Sales Network," with a structure of headquarters, provincial branches, exclusive first-tier wholesalers, second-tier wholesalers, third-tier wholesalers, and end retailers. The operation of this network worked like this: at the beginning of the year, exclusive first-tier wholesalers advanced a payment to Wahaha according to their respective sales volume. Wahaha would pay the wholesalers the interest on the advance payment in accordance with the interest rate of the banks. The first-tier wholesalers had to settle the payment of the last order before getting the delivery of a new order. The first-tier wholesalers could develop their own exclusive second-tier wholesalers or second-level wholesalers. The difference was that an advance payment was required of the former, who, in return, got more benefits. Wahaha developed just one exclusive first-tier wholesaler within a region. It also sent sales and distribution managers to help the first-tier wholesalers with distribution, inventory control, and sales promotion. In some regions, the first-tier distributors only supplied working capital, warehouse, transportation, and logistic services. All the rest of the marketing-related activities were carried out by the Wahaha people. In summary, Wahaha's distribution network was composed of two systems: distributors and Wahaha subsidiaries. The distributors were playing the role of logistic service providers in charge of warehousing and goods delivery, as well as the role of an intermediary to facilitate the working capital and cash flow, while regional subsidiaries were responsible for overall management, services, advertisement, and promotion.

Although exclusive first-tier distributors needed to make advance payment—sometimes as much as several million yuan—they were willing to cooperate with Wahaha. The reasons were: Wahaha was a name brand, and it offered advertisement support; Wahaha offered a full set of product series, making it easier for distributors to lower the cost; and Wahaha featured various benefits for distributors and provided free support through its subsidiaries. Certainly, there were challenges for the exclusive first-tier distributors. In addition to the advance payment to Wahaha, they must work hard to expand the regional market. Otherwise, they might forfeit their status in the United Sales Network.

All of the over 30 provincial subsidiaries and more than 2,500 exclusive first-tier wholesalers reported directly to Zong. This ensured the quick-response mechanism. Through the United Sales Network, Wahaha managed its sales with high efficiency, using only 2,000 salespeople all over the country. It was reported that it took just three days for Wahaha's new product to be distributed into hundreds of thousands of convenience stores and small shops all across the nation.

Wahaha's Future Cola was launched on July 10, 1998—the day of the opening of the World Cup in France. At the prime time before the live TV broadcast of the opening game, Future Cola's advertisement was shown in front of hundreds of millions of Chinese football fans. It marked the start of an intensified ad campaign. The main media was CCTV, for it was most effective in reaching audiences in small towns and rural areas. Together with the advertisement on regional TVs all across the nation, a distinctive message was conveyed to the target customers: drinking a local Chinese Cola symbolized a happy life.

The intensified advertisement campaign, low pricing (RMB 0.5 to 0.6 cheaper than Coke per bottle), and highly effective distribution network made Future Cola a rapid success. Table 1.1 shows sales figures of carbonated drinks, comparing the growing market share of Future Cola with Coke and Pepsi.

Table 1.1   Coke, Pepsi, and Future Cola Sales Compared

Year	Coke (million ton)	Pepsi (million ton)	Future Cola (million ton)
1998	1.94	0.76	0.0738
1999	2.04	0.91	0.399
2000	2.18	1.09	0.48

And in 2001, Future Cola's sales reached 0.595 million tons. The total sales of all drink products of Wahaha reached 2.5 million tons. It matched the sales volume of Coke in the China market.

A Decade of Collaboration with Danone Was in Trouble

Wahaha competed with MNCs. It also collaborated with them. But the collaboration didn't end up well.

In March 1996, Group Danone Asia Pacific President Du Haide (according to Chinese translation) announced the marriage of Danone with Wahaha: "Today, we're so glad to celebrate the birth of a baby—the joint venture we established with five companies of Wahaha. This newborn baby will inherit the good qualities of both the father and mother—an ideal combination of the excellent Chinese and European blood. We believe, under our joint efforts, she will grow healthily . . . "[6] Five companies of Wahaha Group—the Food Company, the Drink Company, the Frozen Food Company,

Healthy Food Company, and Baili Food Company—joined hands with Danone and BNP of Hong Kong. Danone and BNP together invested US$45 million, holding 51% of the shares. The other 49% was held by Wahaha.

Groupe Danone of Paris is a multinational food company covering a wide sphere of business lines. It has operations in over 100 countries in all the six continents of the world. In the late 1980s, Danone entered China and expanded quickly through buying and joint venturing with local companies. It established a yogurt company in Guangzhou. The first China venture grew rapidly and its yogurt products won the market of Guangzhou and Shanghai.

Danone's following expansion moves included:

- In 1992, a joint venture in Shanghai with Shanghai Biscuit Company, holding a 54.2% share.
- In 1994, two joint ventures with Shanghai Bright Dairy & Food Company to produce yogurt and fresh milk products, holding 45.2% of the shares.
- In 1996 (the same year Danone reached the joint venture deal with Wahaha), it bought 54.2% of the shares of Wuhan Donghu Brewery, and established another joint venture, Tangshan Ouliang Haomen Brewery, holding 63.2% of the shares.

In the starting year of the collaboration with Wahaha, the joint venture made RMB 865 million in sales and RMB 111 million in profit. Ten years later in 2006, the sales of the joint venture reached RMB 14 billion with RMB 1.1 billion in profit. The figures obviously showed a very successful cooperation between Wahaha and Danone. However, in May 2007 Danone filed a lawsuit with the Arbitration Institute of the Stockholm Chamber of Commerce, accusing Wahaha Group and three of its subsidiaries of violating the "terms of non-competition" in their joint venture deal by using the "Wahaha" brand without the approval of the joint venture. The accused three companies of Wahaha are not joint ventures with Danone. In their joint venture agreement, Wahaha and Danone promised that the two sides will not engage in any production or marketing activities that may lead to competition with the joint venture's business operation. In case of any dispute that couldn't be resolved by the two sides, they would resort to arbitration with the Arbitration Institute of the Stockholm Chamber of Commerce. After the financial crisis in Asia, the Hong Kong BNP sold its shares of the joint venture to Danone, giving it a controlling stake of 51% of the joint venture. According to Zong's public letter[7] addressed to the board of Groupe Danone on June 7, 2007, Danone's proposal that Wahaha transfer the "Wahaha" brand to the joint venture was overruled by the State Trademark Administration. Then the two sides signed two agreements: one was submitted to the related government administrative organs; the other agreement between the two parties actually acknowledged the brand transfer from Wahaha Group to the Wahaha–Danone joint ventures. According to the latter agreement, the Chinese side could use the "Wahaha" brand for other products upon approval of the board of the joint venture.

Zong wrote in this public letter that Wahaha established 39 joint ventures with Danone since 1996. The total capital investment of the two sides amounted to RMB 3.329 billion. Actual fixed asset investment was RMB 4.439 billion. However, there was still a shortage of RMB 0.88 billion in equipment, land purchase, and plant construction. The gap was all filled by Wahaha alone. And Danone didn't contribute any advanced technology to the joint venture, either. Danone had invested 1.5 billion yuan in the ventures with Wahaha since 1996 and made a combined profit of 3.8 billion yuan.[8] Zong claimed that he had made many proposals to the board of the joint venture on market expansion and new product development, such as increasing the production capacity of bottled water, and building factories in the less-developed western regions of China. But time after time these were turned down by the board. It was after these frequent rejections that Zong chose to implement the above expansion plans through the non–joint venture companies.

Signing the brand usage agreement with Danone was a misstep Zong regretted very much. He should have considered the cost of losing ownership of the brand in exchange for technology and capital from Danone when the agreement was signed. For a rather long period of time, however, Danone seemed to have accepted the operations of Wahaha's non–joint venture companies. The situation changed in April 2007. Danone proposed an acquisition deal of RMB 4 billion to Wahaha for a 51% share of the latter's non–joint venture companies. (By the end of 2006, the total assets of Wahaha's non–joint venture companies had reached RMB 5.6 billion, with annual profit of RMB 1.04 billion.) Zong thought the offer was not fair and rejected it.

When Danone sued Zong for illegal use of the Wahaha Brand, Zong claimed to countersue Danone for violation of anti-monopoly regulation in China. China's booming economy is attracting investment from across the globe, but the challenges are daunting. The government has tightened controls on mergers and acquisitions. According to this regulation, the following benchmarks were used on judging whether foreign investors' merger and acquisition of domestic companies would lead to monopoly: the annual sales revenue surpasses RMB 1.5 billion; acquire more than 10 domestic companies within a year; domestic market share has reached 20%; the acquisition leads to 25% of the domestic market share. "As China has already issued regulations on foreign mergers and acquisitions of Chinese enterprises, the Ministry of Commerce will adhere to these regulations so as to not only encourage foreign investment but also to protect the rights and interests of Chinese businesses," said ministry spokesman Wang Xinpei in answer to a question on Danone's potential acquisition of Wahaha. That was the only response from the government on the issue. "Danone would most likely violate the first item. Whether or not Danone has surpassed the RMB 1.5 billion remains to be confirmed," said one senior legal expert on foreign investment.

In a media interview[9] conducted by Sina.com on April 8, 2007, Zong talked about the joint venture's board meeting held in April. According to Zong, the atmosphere of the negotiation was tense. Zong argued the "term of non-competition" was not fair. It restricted Wahaha from producing competing goods without any restriction on Danone. Over the past years, Danone purchased many companies that produced competitive goods with the Wahaha–Danone joint ventures. As to this complaint, Danone agreed to modify the terms on non-competition.

After Danone's joint venture with Wahaha, it had purchased many companies that had produced competitive goods with the joint venture: in 1998, it purchased a 54.2% share of Shenzhen Health Food Company, which was the first listed mineral water producer in China; in March 2000, it purchased a 95% share of Robust, which produced many competitive products with Wahaha; in 2001, it invested in Shanghai Bright Dairy and Food Company, holding a 5% share; in 2004, it purchased a 50% share of Meilin Zhengguanghe Drinking Water Company; in April 2005, it increased its share of Bright Dairy to 9.7%, becoming the third largest shareholder; in April 2006, its share of Bright Dairy was further increased to 20.01%; in July 2006, it became the second largest shareholder of Huiyuan Group by holding 22.18% of the shares (Huiyuan's main products were fruit drinks); in December 2006, it established a joint venture with Mengniu (Danone held a 49% share of the joint venture, which was engaged in the production, R&D and sale of yogurt products).

With no agreement reached in the board meeting, Danone decide to resort to legal action. Danone filed a lawsuit in Los Angeles seeking more than US$100 million for the alleged illegal sales. The target of the lawsuit was a company controlled or owned by Zong, his wife, and daughter, who are listed as the company's legal representatives and who live in California. Zong was angered by the lawsuit, saying that Danone had used dirty tactics to smear his name and harm his family. Zong resigned as chairman of the joint venture as a protest.

By strict legal terms and the rules of a market economy, it seemed that Danone would definitely win the suit. It's not as simple as that, however. According to Danone, non-joint venture companies started sometime after 2003 and began expanding aggressively, manufacturing a growing share of the Wahaha group's products in 2005. Danone had remained silent for a long time over the usage of the brand by Wahaha's non–joint venture companies. Though Danone had on hand a contract with favorable terms on its behalf, the contract could not solve all the problems in the business operations. It was especially true with an industry such as drinks that lacked a high access threshold and heavily depended on channels of distribution. Brand value is an important asset indeed. But it is inseparable from the existing channels and market. That's why Danone would rather share the brand with the joint venture for the sake of retaining the channels and market.

Danone had largely left managing the business to Zong. Danone admitted it did not have a single executive at Wahaha's Hangzhou headquarters, and it never participated in the joint venture's day-to-day operations.[10] This absence caused the Chinese side to feel it was doing all the work, with all the rewards going to absentee owners. The employee loyalty was clearly steered toward Zong. Danone officials acknowledged that they took a risk on Zong, who is known for his brash management style. But they also said that the 61-year-old entrepreneur helped transform Wahaha into one of China's most successful beverage makers.[11] The question is not so much about whether the foreign partner actively participated in managing day-to-day operations. It is rather a question of perceived contribution to the joint venture. Bringing in cash was perceived as useful in Wahaha's early stage of development for expansion. Having an association with a multinational corporation may also bring certain prestige (not necessarily the brand in this case, since Wahaha is more well-known than Danone in China.) When Zong single-handedly elevated Wahaha to be one of the most valuable brands in China, Zong must have reevaluated the contribution equation.

The case is a blow to Danone's aggressive strategy of piggybacking into new markets. Danone now faces an uphill battle if it is to restore stability to the joint venture, which accounts for 75% of its China operations. The big challenge is how Danone deals with the relationship with Zong. Though Danone has 51% of the equity, the joint venture depends on Zong's continuing cooperation. Not only is he chairman and general manager of the joint venture, but he is the driving force behind the entire Wahaha organization. People associate his name with the Wahaha brand. Winning the court case and pushing out Zong are not perfect solutions. Danone's joint ventures have made Danone move faster in the China market. But effectively managing joint ventures is not an easy task.

Notes

1. December 12, 2007, *International Herald Tribune.*
2. In China, "private-owned enterprises" refers to those that are not state-owned or foreign-owned. They include those that started with private ownership but are now listed as public companies.
3. The Chinese currency is the Renminbi (RMB). The units for RMB are yuan, jiao, and fen. 1 yuan = 10 jiao = 100 fen. Li is 1/10 of fen. One US penny is about 7 fen or one US dollar is about RMB 6.8 in 2008.
4. State Administration of Industry and Commerce.
5. Ministry of Health.
6. *Extraordinary Marketing Strategy*, Wu Xiaobo, p. 143.
7. http://finance.sina.com.cn/chanjing/b/20070607/19313671346.shtml
8. April 11, 2007, *South China Morning Post.*
9. http://finance.sina.com.cn/chanjing/b/20070408/17483482198.shtml
10. June 25, 2007, *The Wall Street Journal Asia.*
11. June 13, 2007, *The New York Times.*

2

Nice

P&G's FIERCE LOCAL COMPETITOR

The dispute between Wahaha and Danone is a high-profile case. In this chapter, we will talk about another local Chinese enterprise that may not be well known outside China, but proves to be a fierce competitor to MNCs in China's detergent market.

P&G entered the China market in 1988 and began to gain profit in 1991. Its sales have been growing at an average annual rate of 50%. By the end of 2003—the fifteenth year of its China operation—P&G announced a new market strategy: "Eagle Shooting Campaign". The "eagle" refers to a local privately owned enterprise—Nice—which used Diao (Chinese pinyin for eagle) as the brand name for its laundry soap and detergent. What kind of a competitor is Nice that makes an MNC such as P&G so nervous as to launch a specific strategy to target it? Let's see how Nice grew from a small rundown factory to a major player occupying more than 40% of China's washing powder market and about 67% of China's soap market.

Product Differentiation: The Rising of a Workshop Factory

Nice Group is located in Lishui in Zhejiang Province. Lack of adequate road infrastructure made Lishui a rather isolated town. When the railway to Lishui came into operation, local people rushed to see what a train was like. Its economic development lagged far behind Wenzhou, another city in Zhejiang.

The predecessor of Nice was a local workshop: Lishui 57 Chemical Factory. The small factory mainly produced laundry soap. It employed only several dozen workers. Its output numbered second last at the bottom of the industry of chemical wash products of the nation.

In March 1992, Lishui 57 Chemical Factory set up a joint venture with Likang Company of Hong Kong. The joint venture was named Nice. It was still a small player in the market. Chairman and general manager of Nice, Zhuang Qichuan, had a similar experience of many young people of the time—being sent to work in the rural areas during the period of Cultural Revolution. He joined 57 Chemical Factory in 1971 as an ordinary worker. He was gradually promoted to a purchasing and sales clerk, head of the purchasing and sales department, and vice director of the factory in charge of operation. When the director of the factory was transferred to another government position in 1985, Zhuang was elected director by the workers of the factory, as the overseeing government organs couldn't find an appropriate person who would like to take charge of such a poorly run factory. After the establishment of Nice, Zhuang decided to make a name in the laundry soap market. There was almost no national brand in this market. They all operated in their own local areas. At that time, laundry soaps were shaped in coarse big rectangular bars of an unappealing yellow color without any packaging. They were nicknamed "smelly soaps" because of the strong smell. But people had to use "smelly soaps" for the laundry. Toilet soaps (called "fragrant soaps" at the time) were pleasant in smell, but they were less effective at dirt cleaning.

Zhuang knew that a market breakthrough must start with a breakthrough in product quality and product design. The first new product Nice developed was the Diao Brand of super-performance laundry soap. With a concave surface in the middle of the bar, the blue-colored new soap looked very different from ordinary Chinese laundry soaps of the time. The brand image of an eagle (called Diao in Chinese pinyin) symbolized rapid and powerful dirt cleaning. When the new soap was launched into the market, however, there wasn't a big splash of market response. Because of the lack of advertisement and promotion, consumers had mistaken the fresh-colored and nice-packaged laundry soap for a toilet soap. To solve this problem, Nice launched a massive advertisement campaign that was very bold and innovative at the time.

On June 21, 1993, Nice's free sample advertisement was covered in Zhejiang Daily. The trademark of a handwritten Chinese character

"Diao" made its first appearance in the media. The advertisement listed the four advantages of Diao super-performance laundry soaps. The readers were told that they could get a bar of super-performance soap as a free sample with the clipping of an advertisement in the newspaper. And the advertisement voucher was also used as a lottery ticket for a free trip to Hong Kong and Macao. The advertisement campaign was a huge success. Free sampling let consumers know the effectiveness of the super-performance soap. Through word of mouth, the Diao brand began to build up a good image among consumers. And the sales of the new soap soared.

Following the success of the super-performance soap, Nice quickly launched another differentiated new product: the Diao Translucent Laundry Soap. It was smaller than an ordinary soap, and easy to hold. The translucent particles added into the soap made it transparent. It had a fresh fragrance because of the use of fragrant additives. The new laundry soap totally differentiated itself from the traditional "smelly soap." In addition, the soap excelled in dirt cleaning and was moderate in price. All these made the translucent soap an immediate success; it still retains a solid consumer base. Although 95% of Chinese urban households have washing machines[1], many of them keep using Diao Translucent Laundry Soap for hand washing clothes.

The success of the super-performance soaps and the translucent laundry soaps earned the first bucket of gold for Nice. By 1994, Nice had become the industry leader, collecting 99.3% of the profit of the whole industry.[2] The Diao brand has since grown beyond the isolated town of Lishui to make its name throughout China.

Winner of the Laundry Detergent Market over P&G and Unilever

With the further opening up and growth of the national economy, the use of washing machines had expanded to over 60% of Chinese households around 1997–98. This brought a structural change to the industry of chemical daily-wash products. Zhuang was smart enough to detect this change. He decided to enter the laundry detergent market.

At that time, China's laundry detergent market was almost monopolized by P&G, Unilever, and a domestic company called Keon. While P&G controlled the urban high-end market, Keon's stronghold was in the huge rural areas, where the MNC giants had not penetrated.

Since Unilever's entrance into China in 1986, it had acquired and merged over a dozen local enterprises in order to expand its business in China. From 1986 to 1999, Unilever's total investment in China reached US$800 million. However, a lack of integration of these various operations led to many problems. Overlapping organizational units and redundant personnel caused increased operational costs. And there even existed competition among its joint ventures.[3]

Between the MNCs' high-end market and local players' low-end market, Zhuang saw an immense vacancy: mid-range products of moderate price and good quality. To improve quality and productivity, Nice imported an advanced production line in 1999.

Nice's traditional approach to detergent advertisements was putting emphasis on product functionality. This time Nice targeted Diao laundry detergent directly at the mid-range market. The advertisement slogan of "Choose what is right, not what is of high price" was launched with an emphasis on good-quality product at a reasonable price. The advertisement won Diao detergent wide popularity among Chinese households and quick brand recognition. Then Nice launched another advertisement featuring family love. It was about a young unemployed mother and her little daughter. The mother went out all day long looking for a job. The thoughtful little girl tried to help the mother by doing the laundry, and with an innocent voice said: "Mother said so much laundry could be done by just a little Diao detergent. It saved us a lot of money!" When the young mother came home at night and kissed her lovely sleeping daughter, she saw the little girl's message: "Mom, I can help you with household work!" Tears welled in the young mother's eyes. This advertisement touched so many people's hearts because it captured the sentiment of the time and reality. The restructuring of big- and medium-sized state-owned enterprises (SOEs), starting in 1998 in China, resulted in a large surplus workforce. The vivid social reality depicted with a deep humanistic touch made the advertisement appeal to a wide audience. It also successfully conveyed the cultural content of Diao brand: family love.

Diao laundry detergent was priced at RMB 29 per box, lower than all the other manufacturers' price of RMB 30 a box. During the May Day holiday period of 2000 (May 1 is a national holiday in China), Nice launched a big promotion by bundling Diao detergent with its translucent soap. The sales of the two product series soared. Market share of the translucent soap rose from 31% in 1999 to over

50% in 2000. The laundry detergent's output grew from less than 100,000 tons in 1999 to 300,000 tons in 2000, capturing the number one market share of the industry. In 2001, Nice's laundry detergent output reached 890,000 tons, five times the total sales volume of all MNCs in China. Its sales volume exceeded the overall sales of all the top 10 manufacturers in the industry. Its sales revenues had also drastically increased from RMB 1 billion in 1999 to RMB 2.5 billion in 2000, and RMB 5.5 billion in 2001.

Nice used similar practices like many other Chinese enterprises; namely, brand promotion through advertisement and market expansion through low price. What made its low-price strategy feasible was its original equipment manufacturing (OEM) production model. In China, 90% of the price of low-value-added products such as laundry detergent went to production and transport. At the beginning, Nice selected over 20 OEMs all over the country to do production. In addition to producing for Nice, these OEMs had actually become its distribution centers. This model saved a lot on transport costs. One interesting thing was that among Nice's OEMs, there were manufacturers with equity stakes by P&G and Henkel. And a Henkel-invested company in Xuzhou turned from losing money into profiting due to producing for Nice. (The Henkel-invested company had suffered a loss of RMB 40 million before producing for Nice.[4])

Zhuang was very impressed with Zong Qinghou's success in Wahaha. He had made several personal visits to Zong and sent people to Wahaha to learn from them. Nice's distribution channel was quite similar to the one used by Wahaha. It also collected advance payment from distributors and provided management support to them through its subsidiaries across the country. In Nice's contract with distributors, it also promised certain benefits at the year end to guarantee reasonable returns for their efforts.

Nice's phenomenal growth caught the attention of MNCs. Their traditional high-end market was close to saturation. Therefore, growth was slow. Most MNCs had not yet made any headway toward the mid- and low-tier market. MNCs began rethinking the importance of a "mid-range strategy." To win the mid-tier market, they had to lower prices. In October 2000, Unilever lowered prices by 40% among its new product series, which caused a chain reaction in the market. At the beginning of 2001, P&G had to counteract with its own price reduction. The price of its Tide and Ariel laundry detergent was cut from RMB 5.9 to RMB 2.2.[5]

The MNCs' new price strategy was also due to strengthened cost control. For example, Unilever restructured its China operations into three parts: household and personal daily care products; food; and drinks and ice-creams. After restructuring, Unilever's sales and distribution resources were integrated. The scale and capacity of its detergent production was expanded. This led to a significant reduction in the cost of its detergent. As a part of Unilever's restructuring, joint ventures were established in Tianjin and Chongqing, which lowered transportation costs by 80%. The restructuring also included new measures on the use of raw materials, leading to marked reductions on material costs. The cost of packaging material was also cut by 20%.

At the end of 2003, P&G participated in CCTV's 2004 bidding for the golden advertisement time slot and won the bid by paying RMB 176 million. In the meantime, P&G made a bold move, announcing a new market strategy targeting directly toward Nice: the Eagle Shooting Campaign.

Move up into the High-End Market

Facing P&G's challenge, Nice took two major measures. One was the establishment of its own production bases and distribution centers. This was to strengthen control on the cost of production and transport and maintain Nice's competitiveness in the low- and mid-range products. In the past several years, the OEM production model had won Nice a head start in scale production and time. But this kind of loose alliance with manufacturers was subject to changes in the market environment. And the OEMs (especially those affiliated with the MNCs) would always have their own interests as the first priority. To solve these potential problems once for all, Nice established five production bases with internationally advanced equipment and technology in the eastern (Zhejiang Province), southern (Hunan Province), south-western (Sichuan Province), northern (Hebei Province) and north-eastern (Jilin Province) parts of China. In the meantime, distribution centers were also set up all across the country. A nationwide production and sales network was thus created.

The other major measure taken by Nice was penetrating into the high-end market. In June 2003, Nice launched a new product series—Diao Brand Natural Soap Powder—designed to be the next-generation product for the current laundry detergent. Although the new product targeted the high-end market of the MNCs, it avoided the mature market of synthesized chemical detergent by combining clothes washing and protection with its focus on the concept of being natural, healthy, and environment friendly: "more suitable for underclothes." Since the production of natural soap powder was not dependent on petrol-chemical materials, it was easy to control the source and cost of raw materials.

Nice employed its usual marketing methods to promote the natural soap powder. It launched extensive TV advertisement across the nation, associating the soap powder with a new concept of clothes washing. Brochures were printed; special promotional items were exhibited on shelves; sales bundled with translucent soaps were launched. However, the market response was not as enthusiastic as when the Diao laundry detergent was launched. It didn't seem possible within a short period of time for the general Chinese consumers to accept a medium- and high-end product such as the natural soap powder as a replacement for the ordinary laundry detergent.

The Diao brand made its name through the slogan of: "Choose what is right, not what is of high price." The widely accepted brand name and distinctive product image had firmly tied Diao to the low- and medium-range market. In addition, its successful product launches in 2001 and 2002—such as Diao toothpaste, shampoo, and body wash—all followed the promotion and sales practices of the low- and medium-range products. It would be hard for Diao's extension into the high-end market to win good market recognition. What's more, it might also harm the Diao brand itself, bringing vagueness to a widely accepted brand position. Considering all these factors, Zhuang decided to use Nice—the name of the company—as the brand name for his high-end products.

In 2004, Nice launched another product for the high-end market—CNICE nutrition toothpaste. The CNICE toothpaste had very innovative packaging—a transparent tube with four colors of blue, white, yellow, and green. Totally different from the old Diao brand toothpaste, it looked very fashionable and high end. In its advertisement, CNICE focused on the new concepts of nutrition, transparency, and fashion. The particular emphasis it put on nutritional value was its differentiating point from other established high-end products such as Colgate and Crest. CNICE was also very selective in distribution channels. It was sold only through supermarkets and shopping malls.

In the war between P&G's "Eagle Shooting Campaign" and Nice's "Eagle Protecting Campaign," each party tried to penetrate into the traditional market stronghold of the other. Nice's magic weapon was its extensive and efficient sales distribution network with a very broad coverage of the rural areas. In the first-tier cities such as Beijing, Shanghai, Guangzhou, and Shenzhou, Nice focused on the supermarkets. In the rest of the country, its distribution was focused on the wholesale market. P&G's advantage was in big cities, controlling the sales terminals of supermarkets and shopping malls. But P&G's market penetration fell far behind Nice in the more extensive and isolated rural markets.

Once Nice had built a solid foundation in the rural areas, it began to compete directly with P&G in big cities. Among its over 100 subsidiaries across the country, Nice set up 30 "terminal offices." (A terminal office, a Chinese terminology, functions as a direct customer account. Nice sells products directly to those supermarket terminals without intermediaries. Supermarkets that sold Nice products were called Nice's "terminals.") These terminal offices were mainly located in provincial capital cities or developed areas. Their major responsibility was to open channels into the cities' super shopping malls such as Carrefour. These terminal offices also reported to the regional subsidiaries and the headquarters' terminal office. Another functional unit in its distribution network was called the "suburbs office." It was also subordinate to the regional subsidiary. In coordination with the terminal office, the suburbs office was in charge of handling the relationship with local agents and distributors for the sake of facilitating the distribution of Nice products in the suburbs.

With an advantage in the high-end market, P&G also began to develop its presence in the markets of small towns and rural areas. In July 1999, P&G launched the "P&G Distribution Plan 2005" in the China market, aimed at reducing the number of small distributors and focusing more on big distributors such as supermarkets and big shopping malls. In 1992, China began gradually opening the retailing industry to foreign investment. The opening up was initially restricted to six pilot cities (Beijing, Shanghai, Tianjin, Guangzhou, Dalian, and Qingdao) and five Special Economic Zones, including Shenzhen, with one or two joint-ventured retailing enterprises allowed for each city. By the end of 1999, only 21 joint ventures of the retailing industry had been officially approved by the government. According to the P&G Distribution Plan 2005, P&G would "tightly control" its distributors, and in the meantime facilitate their transformation. The role of distributors was to be transformed from a middleman who made money out of the price difference of buying and selling into a service provider who earned commission through supplying goods and logistic services. It was reported, as a result of this plan, that P&G's distributors were cut by over 40%.[6] In the second half of 2002, P&G introduced differentiated pricing policies for distributors (such as a 1% payment rebate for those who ordered 1,000 units), which further reduced the number of small distributors.

One distributor of P&G said: "Price-cutting itself would never work for capturing more market share. Compared with foreign brands, local brands earn more profits for distributors. The amount of profit decides whether or not a distributor would devote to the sale of your products."[7] Zhuang had once confessed that for a pack of 300-gram laundry detergent, the manufacturer's profit was less than RMB 0.1. But the distributor's profit could be several times the manufacturer's. P&G relied on large-scale distributors, and distributors had to make big purchases and sales figures to maintain reasonable profits. This model was not a viable option for smaller distributors in the second- and third-tier markets that did not have the economies of scale. P&G's standardized channel operations, highly efficient in mature markets, may not be perceived as flexible by local distributors. Compared with the flexible relationship-building practices of local enterprises, P&G was at a disadvantage in retaining and attracting distributors.

Many MNCs could rapidly win the high-end market after entering China. But they paid less attention to the mid- and low-range market. This left a huge vacuum for local competitors' growth. The success story of Wahaha against Pepsi and Coke in the last chapter and Nice against P&G are good examples of this. In China, there are great differences between major cities and small towns and rural areas. You can attain huge profits in the big cities. But it is small towns and the rural areas that make up the larger market share. What's more, growing Chinese POEs are working hard to move upward along the value chain. After their success in the mid-range market, they often attempt to penetrate into the high-end market and thus create competition for the MNCs. In order to capture bigger market shares, some MNCs have to drop their high-end strategy and offer medium-range products at a relatively low price to fight the local POEs. The competition between MNCs and Chinese local POEs is becoming increasingly fierce in the China market.

Notes

1. http://www.chinaccm.com/48/4809/480902/news/20061214/140118.asp
2. http://www.zj.xinhuanet.com/business/2004-08/03/content_2615464.htm
3. http://www.emkt.com.cn/article/39/3974.html
4. http://www.pma.com.cn/zhuanjia/2007/0814/content_3433.html
5. http://www.cnad.com/html/Article/2004/0528/20040528120020292783
   .shtml
6. http://www.smte.net/Get/CManage/qysj/2005-11/17/110525051117092200
   44211597.html
7. http://news.cnfol.com/060104/101,1609,1625506,00.shtml

CHAPTER

Taobao

THE eBAY KILLER

Bay entered China's market in March 2002 by acquiring the most popular Chinese auction site, EachNet. EachNet.com was founded by two young Chinese Harvard Business School graduates who transported the eBay concept to China in 1999. It had built a registered user base of 3.5 million, with a transaction volume of RMB 780 million (US$97.8 million), and a C2C market share of about 90% before eBay invested US$30 million to buy a 33% stake.[1] And in June 2003, eBay invested another US$150 million to buy the remainder of EachNet. According to eBay CEO Meg Whitman, China held a strategic importance in eBay's global strategy and the company was ready to invest for the long term: five to 10 years payback on its investment would be sufficient.[2]

But only four years later, eBay made a deal that looked like it was retreating from the China market, though eBay said the deal did not represent a pullback.[3] In December 2006, eBay and Tom Online (Tom Group, Hutchison Whampoa's media flagship that provides wireless communications services) announced that Tom would invest US$20 million (a 51% stake) and eBay would invest US$40 million (a 49% stake) to form a new joint venture. eBay EachNet would be incorporated into the new venture (eBay China global trading would be independent), and the new venture in the name of Tom EachNet would be managed by Tom Online.

What happened to make eBay change its mind? At least part of the answer lies at Taobao, a Chinese C2C Web site that was founded when eBay already monopolized China's C2C market with over 90% market share. But according to a market research report released by China Internet Network Information Center in May 2006, the market share of eBay EachNet decreased to 29.1% while Taobao saw its market share increase to 67.3%.

Taobao: Alibaba's Defense

Alibaba's B2B Web site served primarily small- and medium-sized enterprises by connecting global businesses with Chinese manufacturers. Alibaba's initial financing of US$4.5 million came primarily from Goldman Sachs in October 1999. By mid-2000, Alibaba had drawn US$25 million in venture capital from Softbank, Goldman Sachs, and others. By early 2003, Alibaba.com had 1.8 million registered users from more than 200 countries and regions, and RMB 60 billion (US$7.3 billion) in trade. Alibaba.com was named "Best of the web: B2B" by *Forbes* magazine for five years in a row (2000 to 2004). It described itself as "the world's largest marketplace for global trade, and a leading provider of online marketing services for importers and exporters."

In April 2003, Jack Ma, chairman and CEO of Alibaba, convened a secret meeting with seven subordinates in his private lakeside villa in Hangzhou. These seven people, with an average age of 25, became the founders of Taobao.com (taobao means "hunt for treasure" in Chinese). On July 10, Alibaba formally announced the establishment of Taobao.com with an investment of RMB 100 million.

Taobao is brought out as a defensive initiative. When Alibaba spotted the budding of B2C on the platform of eBay, it predicted that eBay would intrude into its B2B realm. To guard against this potential danger, the best policy was to strike back through attacking the opponent's C2C market, and then eBay wouldn't be able to spare any effort to invade Alibaba's B2B market.

Jack Ma's expectation for Taobao was clear: C2C market share rather than profit as a goal. Therefore, from day one of Taobao's inception, the target was eBay EachNet. In the first one or two months of operations, the seven founders worked more than 10 hours every day carefully studying eBay EachNet's site, debating its strengths and weaknesses, totally isolated from the outside world with no access to phones or email.

Differentiation from the Competitor

After a thorough analysis of the competitor's SWOT, Taobao decided it should be different from eBay in several ways:

Free of Charge vs. Service Fees

From free online news to free job posting to free downloads, the word "free" is a norm rather than an anomaly in China's Internet market. At its inception, Jack Ma declared that it would be free of charge for three years. eBay EachNet believes that charging a small fee will be a good barrier to filter out non-serious users and improve the buyer experience by preventing the site from being bombarded with junk listings. However, on May 1, 2005, eBay EachNet scaled back its fee structure to lower the sellers' transaction costs by as much as 75%. After the adjustment, eBay EachNet had the lowest pricing structure within all eBay sites globally. In October 2005, Jack Ma reaffirmed that Taobao would not charge service fees for another three years.

Focus on Buyers

Taobao designed and delivered its services solely to meet the demands of its Chinese customers. From day one, Taobao decided to focus on buyers in the belief that where there are buyers, the sellers will follow. The buyer-focused strategy meant Taobao would make every effort to facilitate the buying process. For example, Taobao employed measures to help buyers find what they needed at the fastest speed, reduce their risks, make it easy for them to judge the credibility of the sellers, and so on. The design of the Taobao front page, product category management, and search engine reflected their understanding of the habits and preferences of their customers.

Alipay vs. Paypal

The lack of a mature personal credit system in China made the security of online payment the most serious concern for Chinese customers. In October 2003, Taobao launched its third-party payment platform, Alipay, based on payment on delivery. After the buyer transferred payment via online banking to Alipay, Alipay would notify the seller to deliver the goods. Only when the buyer received the goods and felt satisfied with the quality would he or she notify Alipay to pay the seller. If the buyer was not satisfied with the goods, he or she could claim a refund from Alipay. Alipay allowed funds to be transmitted through four of China's largest banks, and it became the default online payment platform for e-commerce in China. For example, in 2006, it had over 20 million users who conducted 250,000 trades worth an average of RMB 40 million (US$5.1 million) a day, and more than 200,000 users who were not doing business on Taobao.

Taobao's management felt they had a competitive edge over eBay EachNet through the launch of Alipay. They noticed that some eBay EachNet buyers required sellers to use Alipay for eBay EachNet transactions. Before the launch of Alipay, the transfer of buyers and sellers from eBay EachNet to Taobao was mainly due to its free-of-charge policy and advertising efforts. After Alipay, the added payment security played another important role in attracting more users from eBay EachNet to Taobao.

EachNet introduced a similar online payment mechanism called EasyPay in 2000 and upgraded it in October 2004, renaming it SafePay (An Fu Tong), while eBay launched the Chinese version of PayPal in July 2005. The localized Paypal supported only RMB transactions and didn't allow cross-border transactions. While PayPal's delivery-on-payment mechanism worked well in countries with sound credit systems such as the US, it didn't work as well in China, where fraud is rampant. For example, sellers could get paid without delivering the goods. In September 2006, eBay EachNet dropped PayPal's "refund after payment" process and integrated PayPal with SafePay. While the mechanisms for the new SafePay and Alipay are similar, users seemed to prefer Alipay. Some users attributed their preference to Alipay's seamless integration within the Taobao site, user-friendly design with clear transaction information and account balance, and fast fund transfers.

Buyer–Seller Communication

eBay EachNet's business model determined that it would not allow direct communication between buyers and sellers before the transaction was over. Any communication had to be via the messages on the Web site, and it often took one or two days for one party to reach the other, while the contact information could only be seen after the purchase order was placed. Taobao took a different approach. It launched Taobao Wangwang, an instant messenger in May 2004 for buyers and sellers to conduct real-time communication. Qiao Feng, the Assistant General Manager of Taobao, explained: "There are always some uncertainties in online transactions for both buyers and sellers. Other than concerns over money, there are also questions about the integrity of the person you're doing business with." With Wangwang, you could "talk" with the seller before you made a purchase. Toto Sun, CEO of Taobao, explained: "Historically, Chinese people enjoy combining the experiences of doing business with making friends. You can't separate one from the other. Taobao tries to meet the users' needs for doing business and making friends. Of course, unlike the social Web sites, making friends here is for the sake of doing business." A veteran seller named "Jiaxing Glacier" mentioned that he stays on Wangwang at least eight hours a day. Many of the buyers became his friends after doing business with him.

Unique Corporate Culture

Taobao, given its name, Web design, and customer experience, is perceived as being very Chinese. And while EachNet translates as easy and fun for doing business in Chinese, eBay has no Chinese equivalent. "Taobao" means treasure hunting, something easily remembered by Chinese people without having to make a conscious effort. According to a survey conducted by Taobao, word of mouth played a crucial role in attracting new customers.

Taobao's management enjoys saying they are a Chinese company with Chinese thinking. This is apparent in the design of the Web site, which targets young Chinese users. Taobao's site was perceived as being easier and more fun to use, while eBay EachNet's was perceived as more professional looking.[4] While Americans may value function and utility, Chinese are more attracted to the aesthetic features (colors and pictures are extremely important) and atmosphere. With this in mind, Taobao created a busy and lively shopping atmosphere on its Web site, and as a result, the Taobao site was considered friendly and lively in a Chinese manner.

To emphasize the Chinese experience, Taobao developed a traditional teahouse culture. Informality, congeniality, gregariousness, and familiarity are the features that draw people to the teahouse every day. Taobao's online moderators are called Di Xiao Er, or small shop owners of teahouses, instead of administrators.[5]

Another Chinese touch includes having each employee select a nickname (avatar) from a character in Jin Yong's Kongfu novels. Jin Yong, who is considered a cultural icon, wrote more than 15 Kongfu novels that are wildly popular among China's younger generation. It's not uncommon for fans to read these stories many times and even identify with certain characters or strive to emulate favorite protagonists. Customers often have little problem remembering the nicknames of Taobao employees, and Taobao employees put effort into trying to live up to the roles they have chosen. If customers encounter problems, they only need to type in a nickname in Taobao's instant messenger Wangwang and they are in touch with someone in real time.

"See the world in a handstand" is another unique part of Taobao's corporate culture. The early days of Taobao coincided with the outbreak of SARS in China. The founding members, after working for a long period of time, did handstands as a simple indoor exercise. Gradually, this exercise evolved into a culture of "seeing the world in a handstand and you'll discover something different." Jack Ma told his staff that eBay looked less fearsome when you were upside down.[6] In the workplace, there is a handstand corner for employees to do handstands in their spare time. Every new employee of Taobao had to learn how to do a handstand. If a new employee was unable to do a handstand in their initial training program, his or her department supervisor would do one in his or her place. Qiao Feng said, "The philosophy of 'seeing the world in a handstand' plays an important role in our competitive strategy with eBay EachNet. At the beginning, eBay EachNet was such a giant in terms of both human and financial resources. We didn't have any advantage. How could we compete with it? However, if we looked at it from a different angle, we might find some of its weaknesses. So, when we encountered a tough problem in our competition with eBay EachNet, we would put the problem aside and look at it from different angles. More often than not, we would come up with some solutions."

The Advertisement War

To attract customers to its site, Taobao first tried to advertise on China's major online sites. Taobao soon found that eBay EachNet had spent an undisclosed amount to sign exclusive agreements with major portals such as Sina, Sohu, Netease, and Tom Online. According to eBay CEO Whitman's prediction, the war of the C2C market in China would be over within 18 months.[7] Taobao had no choice but to reach advertising agreements with the Medium and Small Websites Alliance, and its pop-ups came out in thousands of small and medium Web sites. This advertising campaign lasted for about a year. In the meantime, Taobao gradually improved the monitoring system for these advertisements. It traced and counted the daily volume of pop-ups, and how many led to follow-up clicks, how many brought registered customers, and how many resulted in transactions and the volume of transactions. The result turned out to be surprisingly good. It attracted more than a million registered customers.

In April 2004, Sina and Yahoo jointly invested to establish a C2C Web site "1pai.com," and discontinued their exclusive advertising agreements with eBay EachNet. In April 2005, Sohu also discontinued its agreement with eBay EachNet and formed a strategic partnership with Taobao. In the same year, MSN entered the Chinese market and chose Taobao as its partner. The breakthrough came in September 2004 when Taobao launched a large-scale marketing campaign in traditional media (TV, outdoor advertisements, and so on) throughout China's first-tier cities such as Beijing, Shanghai, and Guangzhou. It was the first Internet-based company to conduct such a large-scale promotion in traditional media. Before that, Internet-based companies generally focused on Internet users as their target audiences and considered communication through traditional media to be ineffective. Taobao's move attracted widespread media and public attention and became a major public event. In response, eBay spent US$100 million in 2005 on market development and promotion.[8] "Whatever eBay EachNet needs, we will provide," said Whitman.[9] To compete with Alibaba, eBay has already departed from the formula it has refined since first venturing abroad in 1999. That recipe includes patiently building word-of-mouth recognition of the eBay brand and only gradually spending on marketing. Television advertising usually is considered only in mature markets. eBay EachNet began TV advertising in 2004.

In 2005, Taobao launched advertisements via traditional media in cities such as Nanjing, Chengdu, and Chongqing. While advertising costs in these cities are not as high as in the first-tier cities, the audience was rather receptive. Taobao made similar efforts in cities such as Xi'an in north China, and found they were not suitable for outdoor advertisements. For example, bus posters in these cities would be covered with dirt shortly after their launch. Taobao's promotion via traditional media continued until 2006. Duan Yu pointed out: "We found that a much higher ROI for the internet advertisement is achieved through the simultaneous launch of advertisement via traditional media and the internet, compared with via the internet only."

"When there are two companies launching advertisements via traditional media, the market is quickly expanding," said Duan Yu. With a 90% market share, eBay EachNet's strategy is simply that "whatever you do, I will follow suit with more money until you are wiped out." The campaign war was not limited to traditional media. Taobao used other PR activities. For example, it teamed up with Feng Xiaogang's New Year feature film *A World Without Thieves*, and *Initial D*, starring young pop icon Jay Chou. The props in the films, including those used by actor Andy Lau, were auctioned on Taobao to draw a crowd. There are only two to three New Year feature films each year, and Taobao signed exclusive contracts with all of them.

Huge Market Potential Brought by Big Market Share

Alibaba invested RMB 450 million (U$56.4 million) into Taobao from 2003 to September 2005. It invested another RMB 1 billion (US$125 million) in October 2005. Meanwhile, after having provided three years' free-of-charge services and seen the market share increase, Taobao needed to experiment with a revenue-generating model.

Yahoo and/or Google Models

"There are several clear and proven business models in China's internet industry—the advertisement models for portals and search engines, the charging model for e-commerce. And there are the SMS model and online game model. Taobao will not engage in the SMS and online game models, but the first three offer huge potential for us," said Toto Sun.

Taobao's page views had exceeded 140 million per day, while Sina, China's number one portal, enjoyed a page view of about 300 million per day. Toto said, "Our page view has higher value as it targets buyers while Sina's page view only targets readers. Portal's advertisement model is applicable for us given the huge page view."

Taobao's research found that the distribution of Sina's users was consistent with that of China's Internet users as a whole in terms of both geography and demography. Users visited Sina to read the news and use email. On the other hand, Taobao's users were mainly university students and office employees with three to five years of working experience in big cities. They visited Taobao for information on products they intended to buy or for purchase online. "We believe our ads will have more clicks and generate much higher value than other Web sites," said Duan Yu, Senior Manager of Marketing.

C2C Revenue-Generating Model

Taobao could also adopt eBay EachNet's fee-charging model. Many industry insiders and media attributed Taobao's success to its free-of-charge policy in view of the fact that Chinese customers love free things. They doubted Taobao's prospects once it began to collect fees from users. Yet Toto had his own point of view: buyers or consumers were the most valuable assets for e-commerce Web sites. Sellers would cling to an e-commerce site as long as it attracted a large number of buyers. Toto thought Taobao should be able to survive on the premise that it could provide good services to attract buyers and its charges were reasonable, given that it had 30 million registered users and more than 500,000 sellers. "When we first launched our ad campaigns, many eBay EachNet sellers did turn to Taobao, setting up online shops and making deals occasionally. It took some time to really convert to Taobao, when they found their Taobao shops were making money," said Toto, "For example, one site is free and you can earn RMB 400 a month, while the other site charges you RMB 1,000 a month but you can make RMB 5,000 a month there. Which site will you choose?"

To some extent, Toto's view may be justified. eBay EachNet adjusted its strategy in December 2005, canceling the shop registration fee. One month later, it cancelled the transaction service fee, but the listing fee and some value-added service fees remained. But the effort did not significantly increase its market share.

Taobao could potentially charge value-added service fees in addition to transaction fees. Duan Yu gave an example of offering two or three Wangwang accounts to some sellers for a fee. Those sellers might have accumulated four Diamonds for credit rating and were able to sell 300 items a day, and they might have some special needs. But according to standard service, every shop could only register one Wangwang account, and they may like to pay for a second

Wangwang. And Taobao might develop some market research or customer relationship management tools, which could enable the sellers to know the profiles of the customers who are likely to buy from them, plus price analysis, and market trend analysis. "Many sellers would like to pay for this kind of value-added service," said Duan Yu.

B2C Model

B2C was also a potential model for Taobao. Taobao's data showed traffic was large during weekdays but declined sharply on the weekends. "The decline indicates online shopping still is not the mainstream. What is the mainstream? Shopping malls, hypermarkets and supermarkets. We expect to bring mainstream consumers online when Taobao builds its B2C business. That's how we position our B2C business," said Toto.

The main obstacle to e-commerce was that consumers lacked confidence in it. Traditional retailers had established systems to protect consumers, such as a return policy. Taobao could set up a policy of cash compensation, asking manufacturers to put down deposits with Taobao and use them to compensate consumers in case of a dispute. "B2C has to assure consumers of the same guarantees they would have received in traditional retailing channels," said Toto.

Taobao launched "Taobao Mall" in May 2006, and brands such as iPod, Nokia, Motorola, Logitech, Lenovo, Haier, Samsung, BenQ, and Skyworth joined in. Under its B2C model, Taobao regarded traditional retailers as competitors. Toto said, "For example, if we choose to focus on consumer electronic products, our competitors will be Guomei and the other big retailers selling the same kind of products." For manufacturers and distributors, the costs of using traditional retailers were very high, but also they had little bargaining power. They longed for a lower cost platform, which Taobao was trying to offer. Yet why did manufacturers such as Haier need Taobao's online platform, given most of them had their own Web sites? Toto pointed out that though the manufacturers had tried online marketing, their Web sites had little traffic and no consumers at all.

eBay China or China Piece of a Global eBay

Like many MNCs, eBay's ultimate goal is to be a truly global cross-border trading place through a single online auction marketplace without national boundaries. At the end of 2003, when eBay completed its acquisition of EachNet, it carried out a major platform migration and moved its servers to headquarters in the US in an effort to conform to its global Web site platform.[10] eBay had successfully implemented it in 31 out of its 33 countries. During its platform migration, the speed to access the site was considerably slowed. Sometimes users were unable to log onto the site. The problem of losing the connection in the middle of a transaction also occurred. Some customers were also confused by the design change. As a result, product listings plunged to 250,000, from 780,000 before the switch.[11]

On the positive side, the global platform was seen positively by some professional sellers who stayed loyal to the eBay site because of cross-border trading opportunities. They could reach customers from other countries. Once it was part of the global platform, any request to localize design and functions to the Chinese user preference needed to go through a formal channel. Much of its engineering decision-making was centralized in the US, which made it difficult to quickly push through necessary engineering changes.[12] Chinese Internet users said eBay was slower than Taobao to introduce new applications and new payment services, and some users considered its site less friendly than Taobao, according to Duncan Clark, chairman of consulting and research firm BDA.[13] "I think the top managers of U.S. internet giants are willing to make localized efforts," said Cao Junbo, a senior analyst at iResearch, "but under the current management system, these managers could not always make their own decisions and that's why they always show a slower response to the Chinese market than the local rivals who apparently have more control over their companies in China."[14] While eBay was busy migrating the platform, Taobao took the opportunity to work harder and faster to enhance its site to increase the user experience.

"We recognize that the migration to the global eBay trading platform set us back at a time when our competition was gaining ground," Whitman admitted later. "We have done this in many markets around the world, and it happened seamlessly. This time, we ran into a strong and nimble competitor."[15]

Notes

1. http://tech.sina.com.cn/i/c/2002-03-18/107177.shtml
2. Beijing Youth Newspaper's interview with Meg Whitman in April 2002, http://news.chinabyte.com/41/1604541_1.shtml
3. Vauhini Vara, December 19, 2006, "eBay says Tom Online Deal is not a 'Pullback' from China," http://online.wsj.com/article/SB116657734128155222.html
4. iResearch Inc., China Online Auction Report.
5. This English translation fails to convey the full impact of this title, which in Chinese encapsulates a warm, humble, and witty person who takes delight in serving patrons.
6. Justin Doebele, April 18, 2005, "Standing up to eBay," *Forbes*, 175(8): 50.
7. http://www.chinabyte.com/homepage/219001885661593600/20041117/1876792.shtml
8. Justin Doebele, April 18, 2005, "Standing up to eBay," *Forbes*, 175(8): 50.
9. http://tech.sina.com.cn/i2006-12-21/09331299318.shtml
10. eBay EachNet, http://forums.ebay.com.cn/thread.jspa?threadID=400057626&tstart=0&mod=1095175178637
11. Justin Doebele, April 18, 2005, "Standing up to eBay," *Forbes*, 175(8): 50.
12. Vauhini Vara, December 19, 2006, "eBay says Tom Online Deal is not a 'Pullback' from China," http://online.wsj.com/article/SB116657734128155222.html
13. Mylene Mangalindan, October, 12, 2006, "China may be eBay's latest challenge as local rivals eat into market share," http://online.wsj.com/article/SB116061 293963989984.html
14. Wang Xing, January 24, 2007, "US Icons struggle to find local web model," *China Daily*.
15. Vauhini Vara, December 19, 2006, "eBay says Tom Online Deal is not a 'Pullback' from China," http://online.wsj.com/article/SB116657734128155222.html

CHAPTER

4

Who Are They?

Chinese POEs: MNC's Main Competitors in the China Market

The success stories covered in the previous three chapters naturally lead to one question: who are these local enterprises that grab market shares from the MNCs? Unlike the Chinese SOEs, most of them started from scratch, and they grew all by themselves without financial or policy support from the government. They are the Chinese private-owned enterprises. Their rapid growth into a major economic power in China is due to the reform and opening-up policy. They are forging the engine of China's economy, and are increasingly becoming MNC's main competitors in the China market.

Table 4.1 lists the competition between MNCs and their main competitors—all Chinese POEs—in the China market.

Small- and Medium-Sized POEs: Your Potential Rivals

The tough competition MNCs face from local well-established POEs is a matter of fact. These leading local POEs, whether of the consumer products, heavy machinery, or hi-tech industries, have mostly grown for about 20 years. Stories and cases of their success are widely covered by media and constantly cited by research institutes and business schools. As public listed companies, these big POEs need to publicize their operations and strategies. MNCs have various channels to find out about them when they realize the importance of the knowledge in winning the China market.

39

Table 4.1   MNCs and their Main Competitors in China

MNC	Main Competitor in China	Market Share
Google September 2000: launched Chinese search service; May 2005: set up the Shanghai office and moved into the China market; April 2006: named itself in Chinese—"Guge"—meaning "Song of Harvest".	**Baidu** 1999: Baidu was established; 2002: search engine technology became mature; 2003: page view increased by seven times over last year; 2004: the brand was widely recognized by Internet users in China; August 2005: listed on NASDAQ	The data provided by Analysys International, an Internet research institute in China, show that Baidu led China's Internet search engine market with 60.1% market share in the last quarter of 2007, while Google was second with 25.9% market share.
HP 1985: established the first hi-tech joint venture in China; 1996: personal computer department was established in HP's China operation, and began turning out personal computers for the local market; July 2002: HP China merged with Compaq; September 2005: HP changed its nation-wide chief agent distribution channel strategy to a system consisting of several regional major agents.	**Lenovo** November 1984: founded by 11 researchers of the Chinese Academy of Sciences with RMB 200,000, with sales of personal computers made by HP and Toshiba as its main business; 1990: Lenovo's first PC was launched to market. It transformed from a sales agent into a producer and seller of its own brand; 1994: listed on the Hong Kong Exchanges and Clearing; 1996: became the number one market leader in China; 2004: acquired IBM's PC division and became world's third largest PC supplier.	According to IDC statistics, in the fourth quarter of 2007, Lenovo led the Asian market (excluding Japan) by a market share of 19.6%, HP held second place with 13.8%, Dell held third place with 8.4%. Lenovo led the China market with 28.8% market share, followed by HP with 10.7% market share.
Dell February 1998: entered China and used its global direct sale channel strategy; September 2007: began using big local household electronics retailers as another sales channel.		

Table 4.1   (Continued)

MNC	Main Competitor in China	Market Share
Siemens Household Electronics December 1994: moved into China by setting up a joint venture with Bosch and Little Swan in Wuxi. The JV produced washing machines bearing the brand of Siemens and Little Swan. Siemens washing machines were for the high-end market, while Little Swan's target customer was medium range. Since there were few Chinese consumers at that time who could afford tumble washing machines, it didn't earn any profit until 1998. March 1996: acquired 70% shares of Yangzi Washing Machine Factory with Bosch and set up a JV producing Siemens refrigerators for the local market. Yangzi brand was abandoned. But Siemens had yet to be accepted by the local consumers. And there were problems in merging with the local partner. All these led to a huge loss for the JV. July 2000, acquired all of the shares of its Chinese partner with Bosch and became wholly owned. It turned a profit in 2001.	**Haier** Haier originated from a state-owned refrigerator factory in Qingdao. The factory was operating at a loss when Mr Zhang Ruimin became the director in 1984. 1985: introduced the technology and equipment of the German Liebherr; 1988: won first place in national quality brand appraisal through its quality control and brand strategy. Haier had since become a well-known brand; 1991: merged another two state-owned enterprises and established QindaoHerr Group; September 1993: renamed the group as Haier Group with the main product line in refrigeration equipment. In the same year, its subsidiary Qingdao Haier got listed in Shanghai Stock Exchange; 1995: merged a local washing machine producer and entered the washing machine market; September 1997: set up a joint venture with the West Lake Electronics Group of Hangzhou and began producing TVs and VCDs;	According to ZDC's (a local research institute on Chinese consumers) survey, in the third quarter of 2007, Haier led the local washing machine market with 48.2% market attention. Siemens held second place with 12.2% market attention. According to "the White Paper on Refrigerator Market 2006" released by the State Information Center, Haier was the market leader with 23.32% market share. Siemens had the second highest market share with 12.16%.

Table 4.1 *(Continued)*

MNC	Main Competitor in China	Market Share
Cisco 1994: opened Beijing office and moved into China; 1998: established wholly owned Cisco Systems (China) Networking Technology Co., Ltd., and announced a planned investment of US$100 million in the next two years; Cisco supplied advanced switches and routers to major Chinese telecom operators, including China Telecom, China Unicom, and China Mobile; 1998: Cisco worked with Fudan University to found the first Cisco Networking Academy in China. By August 2006, it had set up over 220 Cisco Networking Academies across China and had trained more than 30,000 networking professionals for China.	April 1999: established production base in North Carolina in the US. In the same year, Haier became the most valued brand of China's household electronics industry with the brand evaluation worth of RMB 26.5 billion; 2004: Haier was listed as one of the "World's Top 100 Brands." **Huawei** 1988: Huawei was founded by seven researchers with RMB 20,000, and supplied telecom equipment to local customers at a price lower than international competitors; 2000: Huawei's overseas sales surpassed US$100 million. It set up an R&D center in Silicon Valley and Dallas; 2002: Huawei acquired Alcatel's joint venture—Shanghai Bell—and became the biggest local supplier of digital switches and routers; 2003: established a joint venture with 3Com and produced corporate digital network equipment; 2004: established a joint venture with Siemens and developed the mobile telecom technology—TD-SCDMA—for the China market;	According to the statistics of CRC-Pinnacle Consulting, Huawei led the 2005 telecom equipment market of China with a market share of 13.5%. Cisco ranked No.11 with a market share of 4%. According to a survey conducted by Analysys International, Huawei led the switch market, followed by the number two player Cisco in the fourth quarter of 2006, while in the router market Cisco was the number one player followed by Huawei.

Table 4.1 (*Continued*)

MNC	Main Competitor in China	Market Share
2005: established a China R&D Center in Shanghai. By 2007, it had become Cisco's biggest R&D center outside the US.	2005: became the preferred supplier of telecom equipment for Vodafone, and achieved a sales volume of US$6.7 billion, 60% of which came from the international market.	
Putzmeister	**Sany Heavy Industry**	In 2004–05, Putzmeister's Chinese market share dropped to 6% to 8%, which was mostly in the high-end truck-mounted concrete pumps. In 2006, Sany's domestic market share of truck-mounted concrete pumps was over 55% and it became one of the world's top three concrete pump manufacturers along with Putzmeister and Schwing.
Before the mid-1990s: China's concrete machinery market was monopolized by Putzmeister and Schwing;	1989: four technological talents of material science education background with one of their friends founded Hunan Lianyuan Weldering Material Factory. The first year sales were RMB 1 million;	
1995: Putzmeister entered China by setting up the wholly owned Putzmeister Machinery (Shanghai), the center of management, production, sales, and after-sales service in the Asia-Pacific region	1991: sales of the factory's special soldering material were among the national top three, reaching over RMB 100 million. The factory was renamed Hunan Sany Group;	
	1994: renamed as Sany Group. Two of its subsidiaries—Sany Heavy Industry and Sany Material Industry—entered the construction engineering machinery sector. The first open type hydraulic system trailer-mounted concrete pump was developed and launched into market in the same year;	

Table 4.1 (*Continued*)

MNC	Main Competitor in China	Market Share
	1995: Hydraulic control system was developed and launched into market. Its production cost was much lower than international competitors; 2000: the world's first full hydraulic motor grader was developed. Sany was ranked number one in overall competitiveness among Chinese enterprises in the engineering machinery industry; 2001: the world's first hydrostatic transmission motor grader was developed; 2003: Sany Heavy Industry was listed on Shanghai Stock Exchange.	
LG Electronics 1993: entered China; 1995: set up a joint venture in Tianjin; 1997–2004: through the "strategic loss" strategy, LG's microwave oven market share in China climbed from 10% to 30%, and became the only foreign brand that could pose a strong competition against the domestic Galanz; 2006: began cutting its microwave oven business in China due to the huge loss caused by price war. Now LG has withdrawn from the microwave oven market in China.	**Galanz** 1978: Galanz's predecessor, a township workshop of down products with 200 employees, was founded. It supplied manually laundered down feather to companies engaged in foreign trade for export. The first-year sales were RMB 470,000; 1987: the workshop invested in two joint ventures, with a Hong Kong company and a US company, making down clothing and quilt for export, respectively. The annual sales were over RMB 100 million; 1992: renamed Galanz Industry (Group) Company. Domestic sales of Galanz down products were RMB 30 million. Sales for export were US23 million;	According to a domestic market survey conducted by China Market Monitor on the third quarter of 2007, local producers took all the top five positions of the microwave oven market. Galanz held 46% market share. Number two was the domestic Midea, holding a 40% share.

Table 4.1   (Continued)

MNC	Main Competitor in China	Market Share
	1993: trial-produced 10,000 microwave ovens and began turning to small household appliances;	
	1995: Galanz's microwave oven output reached 250,000, holding 25% domestic market share, and it became one of the domestic market leaders;	
	1996: initiated a price war with 40% price cut. Its market share rose to 34.7%;	
	1997: further cut prices by 29% to 40% and captured 47.6% market share. It had since become the number one market leader;	
	1998: Galanz's microwave oven output reached 4.5 million and it became the world's biggest microwave oven producer;	
	1999: established a North America branch and an R&D center in the US. The annual sales reached RMB 2.96 billion, in which 50% was from domestic market and 50% was from export. Its domestic market share was 67.1%; European market share was 25%;	
	2005: Galanz produced 20 million microwave ovens. Galanz is the OEM for over 200 international companies. Only 20% of microwave ovens it produced bear the Galanz brand. However, Galanz has set a goal for its future development—to transform from a "world factory" into a "world brand."	

There is another group of local players in the China market, however, which the MNCs have to know about for a sustainable operation in China. They have not become so well known as the abovementioned local players. MNCs know little about them. But they share most of the essential qualities of the leading local players that win the competition against MNCs. They understand Chinese consumers. They are quick to adapt and resolute in taking risks. They believe in the wisdom of the "starting from countryside, then penetrating into cities" strategy, a most acclaimed guideline of Mao Zedong's guerrilla war strategy in the anti-Japanese war. They start with the low-end market (often in China's rural areas), move into the mid-range (often in China's urban areas) once a segment vacancy is spotted, and prepare themselves for the upper end and enter it when they are ready. Who are they? They are the fast-growing small- and medium-size Chinese POEs—the focus of study and analysis in this book. They are undergoing a similar process as the nowadays well-established Chinese POEs—the main competitors of MNCs in the China market. And some of them promise an even brighter future than their compatriot forerunners. The purpose of this book is not only decoding the make-up of the existing tough local competitors, but also understanding the potential rivalry from these fast-growing small businesses.

As individual economic entities, most of the Chinese POEs are small-sized and are in the stages of growing up. But it is these "small potatoes" that play a major dynamic role in the rapid economic development of China. According to National Bureau of Statistics of China (NBS), by the year 2005 China's POEs had contributed half of China's GDP, over three-quarters of the export and import volume, and more than 75% of the urban employment.[1] The target readers of this book are those who are interested in the study of the Chinese economy or those who are engaged in business activities in the China market, helping them gain a deep understanding of the Chinese POEs and their founders—the Chinese startup entrepreneurs.

We conducted in-depth face-to-face interviews with 20 Chinese POE entrepreneurs (see Appendix A for a list of the questions that were asked, and Appendix B for the companies involved). They are selected based on the following set of criteria: the entrepreneurs must start from scratch, without any special family background both in terms of significant political influence and economic support;

the private enterprises must be in business for at least five years; and the entrepreneurs and their enterprises haven't received much media exposure. In addition to that, we also take into consideration the diversification of industries and geographic regions.

Research Methodology

Our research involved interviews with 20 entrepreneurs—their businesses are (in alphabetical order): Aiminger Leather Products, Bridge HR, Compass Global Freight, Dynaforge Tools & Hardware, Eitong Air Express, Essence Technology Solution, Hightex, KeyPoint Controls, Longtaixiang Metal Products, Merryland Real Estate Development, Opple Lighting, Original Enterprise, Runway Technology, Speedup Automobile Racing Club, SPN Technology, Tony's Group, Wangu Textile, Xhan Yang Chemical, Zhicheng Communication, and Zhongxin Chemical. These enterprises represent more than a dozen industries, including communications software, chemicals, cable, equipment and meters for automated control, engineering machinery, real estate, hardware and tools, shoe manufacturing, lighting fixtures, textiles, international cargo transport, express delivery, and employment services. Most fall into the category of tertiary industry, and a few manufacturers are in secondary industry. Although these entrepreneurs all hail from various provinces and municipalities, half of them began their business in Shanghai and only two are native Shanghainese. Of the 20 subjects, five are female. Most of the interviewees were born in the 1960s and a few in the early 1970s, 14 have college degrees including three with Master's degrees, and most earned an EMBA once their businesses were established.

Interviews included questions about strategy, management and organization, as well as questions specific to Chinese POEs, such as how they first struck gold, and problems such as obtaining financing. Generally speaking, our interview questions can be classified into five types—they are:

- Personal background and career experience before embarking on business
- The start-up of the enterprise
- The enterprise's development path
- Agency problems
- Personality characteristics

All the featured information regarding these subjects derives from our interviews. The presentation of this information is displayed in a matrix structure—topics are arranged horizontally and people and events arranged vertically. This allows the reader to see how these 20 entrepreneurs and enterprises are similar and how they differ in their responses to similar situations, offering insight into their reasoning.

Part II begins with a chapter on the history of Chinese commerce, introducing the evolution of business awareness, entrepreneurship, and management concepts of Chinese merchants. It details the advanced business acumen of long-ago merchants, including the recall of inferior products as a part of a marketing strategy 200 years ago, and understanding the importance of brand building and R&D 100 years ago, as well as using incentives such as bonuses, pensions, and survivor's pensions. The chapter will illustrate how China has had a long history of entrepreneurship, and that the Cultural Revolution in the 1960s and 1970s temporarily suspended the evolution of Chinese business traditions.

The Role of POEs in China's Economy

Contributing Half of the GDP

In 2005, POEs contributed 49.7% of the GDP (see Table 4.2).[2]

In 2006, the number of POEs was 57.4% of the total number of enterprises in China (see Table 4.3 and Figure 4.1).[3]

Table 4.2   2005: The Contribution of POEs

	Primary Industry	Secondary Industry		Tertiary Industry
		Industry	Construction	
Contribution of POEs in three industries	92.0%	38.8%	69.1%	41.0%
Contribution of POEs to GDP in three industries	14.0%	17.8%	4.8%	13.1%

Source: *Blue Book of Non-State-Owned Economy 2005–2006.*

In 2006, POEs contributed 51.6% of the total investment in fixed assets in urban areas.[4] Table 4.4 shows investment in fixed assets from 2000 to 2005.

Figure 4.2 shows investment in fixed assets from SOEs and POEs.

In 2005, the export and import volume of POEs was 77.8% of the national total (see Table 4.5 and Figure 4.3).

Table 4.3   The Growth of POEs

	2000	2001	2002	2003	2004	2005	2006
The number of registered POEs (million)	1.76	2.03	2.44	3.01	3.65	4.30	4.98
Registered capital (100 million)	13,308	18,212	24,756	35,305	47,936	61,331	76,029

Source: State Administration for Industry & Commerce.

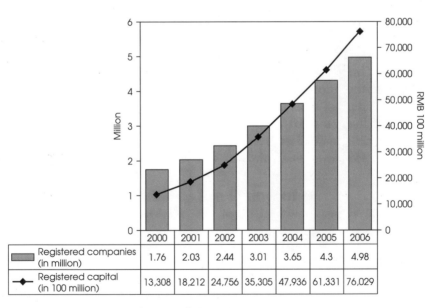

	2000	2001	2002	2003	2004	2005	2006
Registered companies (in million)	1.76	2.03	2.44	3.01	3.65	4.3	4.98
Registered capital (in 100 million)	13,308	18,212	24,756	35,305	47,936	61,331	76,029

Figure 4.1   Growth of Private Enterprises
Source: State Administration for Industry & Commerce.

Table 4.4   Investment in Fixed Assets: Decreased Contribution from SOEs vs. Increased Contribution from POEs

	2000	2001	2002	2003	2004	2005
SOEs	50.1%	47.3%	43.4%	39.0%	35.5%	30.6%
FIEs	7.9%	8.1%	7.9%	8.8%	9.9%	9.4%
POEs	41.9%	44.6%	48.7%	52.2%	54.6%	60.0%

Source: National Bureau of Statistics.

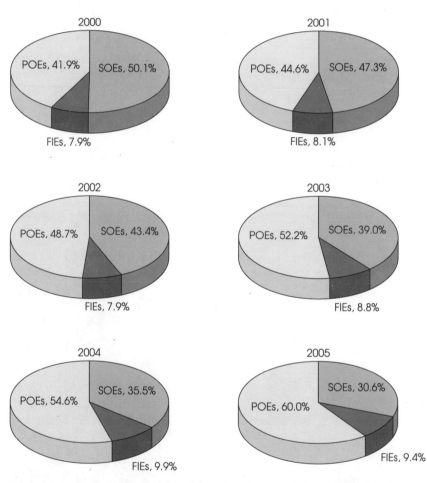

Figure 4.2   Investment in Fixed Assets: Decreased Contribution from SOEs vs. Increased Contribution from POEs

Source: National Bureau of Statistics.

Table 4.5 POEs: Main Exporter[5]

	2000	2001	2002	2003	2004	2005
POEs' export volume (US$100 million)	1,327.6	1,529.2	2,027.0	3,003.3	4,397.6	5,931.9
Export of POEs / China's total export	53.3%	57.5%	62.3%	68.5%	74.1%	77.8%

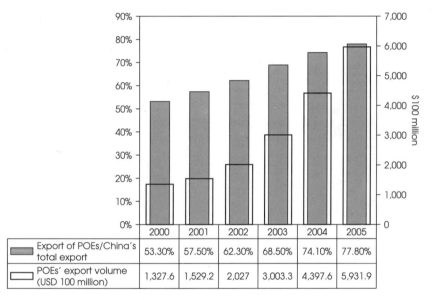

	2000	2001	2002	2003	2004	2005
Export of POEs/China's total export	53.30%	57.50%	62.30%	68.50%	74.10%	77.80%
POEs' export volume (USD 100 million)	1,327.6	1,529.2	2,027	3,003.3	4,397.6	5,931.9

Figure 4.3 POEs: Main Exporter

Source: *Blue Book of Non-State-Owned Economy 2005–2006.*

A Main Channel of Employment in China

In 2005, the number of persons employed by urban POEs reached 207 million. In the same period, the number of persons employed in the state sector was 64.88 million (see Table 4.6 and Figure 4.4).[6]

Table 4.6 Employer of 3/4 Urban Residents

	2000	2001	2002	2003	2004	2005
Employment in urban POEs (million)	150.49	163.00	176.17	187.63	197.66	207.00
Employment in urban POEs / Total urban employment	65.0%	68.1%	71.1%	73.2%	74.7%	75.8%

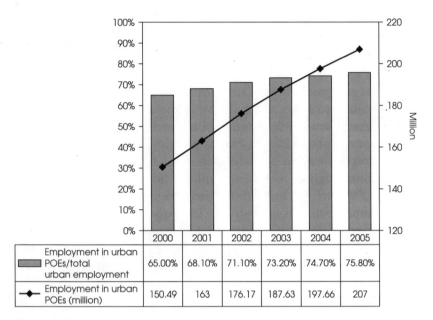

	2000	2001	2002	2003	2004	2005
Employment in urban POEs/total urban employment	65.00%	68.10%	71.10%	73.20%	74.70%	75.80%
Employment in urban POEs (million)	150.49	163	176.17	187.63	197.66	207

Figure 4.4   Employer of 3/4 urban residents

Source: *Blue Book of Non-State-Owned Economy 2005–2006.*

A Main Contributor of Fiscal Revenue

In 2005, tax paid by POEs reached RMB 2 trillion and RMB 337.79 billion, 75.7% of the national total (see Table 4.7 and Figure 4.5).[7]

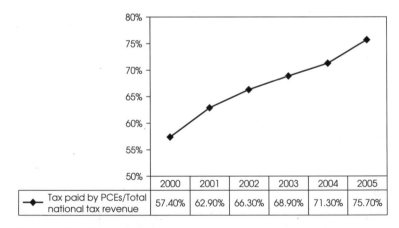

	2000	2001	2002	2003	2004	2005
Tax paid by PCEs/Total national tax revenue	57.40%	62.90%	66.30%	68.90%	71.30%	75.70%

Figure 4.5   Major Tax Payer

Table 4.7 Major Tax Payer

	2000	2001	2002	2003	2004	2005
Tax paid by POEs / Total national tax revenue	57.4%	62.9%	66.3%	68.9%	71.3%	75.7%

Source: State Administration for Industry & Commerce; *Blue Book of Non-State-Owned Economy 2005–2006.*

Notes

1. *The Development Report of Non-State-owned Economy in China.*
2. *Blue Book of Non-State-Owned Economy 2005–2006,* All-China Federation of Industry & Commerce.
3. Source: State Administration for Industry & Commerce.
4. Source: National Bureau of Statistics.
5. *Blue Book of Non-State-Owned Economy 2005–2006,* All-China Federation of Industry & Commerce.
6. *Blue Book of Non-State-Owned Economy 2005–2006,* All-China Federation of Industry & Commerce.
7. *Blue Book of Non-State-Owned Economy 2005–2006,* All-China Federation of Industry & Commerce.

PART

II

THE EVOLVEMENT OF ENTREPRENEURSHIP IN CHINA

CHAPTER 5

The Development of Chinese Commerce

A Brief Historical Background

As far back in history as the early 15th century BC, examples of capitalism can be found in China. During the first slave dynasty, Xia (2050 BC to 1600 BC), tribal chief Wanghai loaded an ox cart and led his tribe to engage in barter trade with other tribes for daily necessities and tools. Wanghai has since been considered "the ancestor of Chinese merchants." In the Shang Dynasty (1600 BC to 1046 BC), the Chinese began using shells as currency, and later in the dynasty saw the emergence of copper coins.

In the second century BC, with the dispatch of Chang Chhian[1] to the Western Regions[2] and the opening of the Silk Road, trade and cultural exchanges between China and the West developed rapidly. This made the Western Region, the area that cut across the Silk Road joining Asia and Europe, a highly strategic area over which the Han Dynasty and Xiongnu[3] long vied for control. In 139 BC, the West Han Dynasty's Emperor Hanwu dispatched Chang Chhian as an envoy to seek allies against Xiongnu. Instead, Xiongnu captured Chang Chhian and his assistants and held them captive for over 10 years. When Chang Chhian and his group finally escaped and returned to the emperor, they did so by way of Ferghana (in the eastern part of Uzbekistan), Taklimakan, and Bactrian. They brought back detailed information about the civilization and development of the region, prompting the first envoy in Chinese history being sent to the Western Region to form diplomatic relations. Chang Chhian was sent a second time to the Western Region in 119 BC; his mission this time was to promote trade and cultural exchanges. It took him four years to visit countries such as Ferghana, Taklimakan, Bactrian, Kangju (along the lower reaches of Syr Darya in Kazakhstan), Parthia (modern Iran), and Shendu (modern Indian subcontinent).

In the following years, the imperial government of the Han Dynasty sent five to 12 envoys annually to the Western Region, each consisting of several hundred people. Chinese products such as silk were taken to the area for trade in exchange for products such as thoroughbred animals, wine, guava, glazed tiles, and wool. Many of those who joined these missions did so voluntarily and were merchants of low status. Most of them made a fortune from these trading expeditions, prompting many more people to enter the business of trading via the Silk Road. Trade then expanded to South East Asia, India, Sri Lanka, the Middle East, Africa, and Europe. Roman historian Florus described how delegations from China met with the founding king of the Roman Empire Augustus. The Romans were so fascinated by Chinese silk that a pound of silk once sold for as much as 12 liang[4] of gold. Visits by the Romans to China were also recorded in Chinese history books.

By the Ming Dynasty (1368 AD to 1644 AD), in addition to overland exchanges, maritime trade also developed enormously. This ended temporarily when the founding emperor of the Ming Dynasty adopted a policy of interior stabilization and sea closures to consolidate his reign. However, after the third emperor Chheng Tsu (Cheng Zu) seized power from his uncle, he undertook an opening-up policy, and once the sea closure was lifted, commercial and trade activities were encouraged. In 1405, Emperor Chheng Tsu dispatched Cheng Ho (Zheng He) on a major westward expedition. Carrying vast amounts of gold, silk, and other treasures—with a fleet of 62 junks with 27,800 officers and men—Cheng Ho sailed to South East Asia and the Indian Ocean, visiting Champa, Java, Sumatra, and Calcutta, returning in 1407. It was Cheng Ho's first of seven such expeditions from 1405 to 1433, which took him as far as Africa, the Red Sea, and Mecca. In addition to trade and exploration, these expeditions made known to the world the existence of the Middle Kingdom and the Son of Heaven, and spread word of his majesty and virtue.

Cheng Ho's expeditions involved three kinds of trade: tribute trade, official trade, and private trade. Tribute trade was aimed at winning other countries' recognition of the Ming Dynasty. Many countries dispatched tribute-bearing missions to the Chinese court to gain its protection as well as rewards. During Emperor Chheng Tsu's 22 years of rule, the number of foreign missionary visits resulting from Cheng Ho's expeditions totaled 318, an average of 15 visits a year. Official trade referred to transactions with local merchants that were hosted by officials from both parties. This was an important way of promoting overseas trade during this period and could be either a barter transaction or one using Ming currency. The most widely accepted way of setting prices was handclapping bidding where the two parties negotiated a price in the presence of officials. Once the price was agreed, the two parties clapped hands with each other signaling they would not renege. Chinese currency thus circulated in various countries; for example, coins made in Zhangzhou (in China's Fujian Province) were used in Banten and Java. Private trade was voluntarily conducted. Because Cheng Ho did not forbid his men from bringing along Chinese merchandise to trade, the Chinese fleets were quite popular as they sailed into ports along their route, especially once Chinese silk and porcelain goods became highly valued in South East Asia. Some of Cheng Ho's men were even invited to local markets to sell their goods, which were traded for jewelry, spices, and herbal medicines. The men could buy pepper at one liang of gold and sell it at 20 liang upon their return to China.

During this time, domestic commerce also flourished. Ten major merchant groups eventually formed, the most prominent being Anhui and Shanxi merchants.

Anhui Merchants

Traditionally in China, social ranking according to occupation put officials at the top followed by farmers, craftsmen, and merchants. People became officials only after long study and passing an imperial examination. But in Huizhou[5] merchants have long enjoyed a higher status than scholars (becoming a scholar and being selected as an official was the only way for commoners to reach such status).

Anhui merchants were involved in various businesses, the main ones being the trade of salt, tea, and wood as well as the operation of pawnshops. According to records, most of the 500 pawnshops in Jinling (the capital during the Ming Dynasty) were run by Anhui merchants. They ran pawnshops even in small rural towns. They also dominated in the trade of wood due to the abundant resources in Huizhou. Initially, such trade involved the exchange of wood for food in neighboring areas, but during the Ming Dynasty this was expanded to Sichuan, Guizhou, Jiangxi, and Hunan through the utilization of water routes as a means of transporting the wood. Wood was in strong demand during the Ming and Qing Dynasties, which saw the rapid development of the ship-building industry. In addition to common ships and battle ships, special vessels were built for the government's transportation of grain; these were called Cao ships.[6] During this period, China's economic center was in the south and its political center was in the north. Every year, the grain transported from the south to the northern capital amounted to several million dan.[7] During the reign of the Ming Dynasty's 15th emperor, the number of Cao ships reached 11,700. Many Huizhou wood merchants made huge fortunes in supplying wood for the royal court. In Emperor Chong Zhen's[8] period, a Huizhou wood merchant named Liao Tingxun gained the business of wood procurement for the construction of the royal mausoleum, and was thus nicknamed a "royal merchant."

The involvement of Huizhou merchants in Beijing's tea market dates back to the Ming Dynasty, and by the Qing Dynasty Huizhou tea merchants held a virtual monopoly in the capital city. Tea played a significant role in the daily lives of royalty. Much time was spent in teahouses, where they drank tea, chatted, and watched Beijing opera. This created a huge market for tea in Beijing, bigger than in other cities. In 1757, Emperor Qianlong closed foreign trade in all ports except Guangzhou with his "one single port of entry" edict, prompting Huizhou tea merchants to move their business to the southern port. In 1843, with the Qing government's "five ports of entry" foreign trade policy, Huizhou tea merchants again moved their business to the biggest market of the time—Shanghai. And Shanghai overtook Guangzhou's ranking as the biggest tea-trading port in China. Huizhou tea merchants were also skilled at developing new products to suit a particular market. For example, the water in Beijing was known for being slightly bitter, but when one Huizhou tea merchant heard that someone had accidentally put jasmine flowers into tea leaves and found that it hid the bitter flavor, he mass-produced jasmine tea and sold it in Beijing.

During the transition between the Ming and Qing Dynasties, China began exporting tea to European countries such as Holland, Switzerland, Spain, France, and Denmark. By the end of the 17th century, tea drinking had become fashionable among people from all social classes in Britain, creating a huge demand for tea internationally. The 18th century, later known as the "Tea Century," saw Chinese annual tea exports to Europe reach 240,000 dan (one dan equals 50 kg); one-third of that was destined for Britain alone. In the later years of Emperor Qianlong's rule, China's foreign trade surplus totaled 850,000 liang of silver.

Despite the wealth earned in tea and wood, the richest Anhui merchants were in the salt business. During Emperor Qianlong's period, the total capital of Huizhou salt merchants equaled the annual revenues of the whole country. Salt merchants in Yangzhou,[9] for example, had assets worth 400,000 to 500,000 liang of silver, while during the most prosperous period of the Qing Dynasty the state treasury had no more than 700,000 liang of silver. During the Ming and Qing Dynasties, the salt trade was administered by the government and the tax collected on salt was a main source of revenue. During Emperor Shenzong's (13th emperor of the Ming Dynasty) period, tax from the salt trade accounted for half of the state's total revenue. Half of the tax came from the Huaihe River[10] area, where Huizhou merchants played a dominant role.

As the salt trade was under the control of government, the merchants had to curry favor with officials to enter this highly lucrative business. Anhui merchants were much more generous than other groups in spending money on bribing officials. They paid all the daily expenses of salt trade officials. One time, an official expressed a fondness for an antique collection and an Anhui salt trader footed his shopping bill of 16,000 liang of silver. Of course, most of the money spent generated handsome returns. A number of Anhui merchants were even given official titles, becoming "red-hat merchants."[11]

The Huizhou merchants' hold on the salt trade eventually rendered the salt trade a monopoly. In the early days of Emperor Daoguang (8th emperor of the Qing Dynasty), profits from the salt trade were enormous. A producer's price was no more than 17 wen[12] plus tax. After it was transported inland, the selling price was between 50 and 60 wen, and reached even higher the further the salt traveled.

In addition to their relationship with officials, Anhui merchants can attribute their 400-year success in commercial activities to other factors. They share a strong clansmanship. Once a Huizhou merchant settles in a certain place, he is almost certainly followed by his relatives and others from his native township. This kind of commercial network based on family and clansmanship allows them to pool their financial, material, and human resources together and build a strong competitive advantage. Their sense of solidarity is apparent in their formation of the Anhui Merchants' Guildhall, which serves various functions such as coordinating with the government on business issues, welfare activities, education, and the delivery of private letters and government proclamations concerning the people of Anhui. Anhui Merchants' Guildhalls were established all over China in the Ming and Qing Dynasties.

Anhui merchants are also reputed for their tenacity, known for "not giving up even if they have failed three times." One story illustrates this trait. A fabric store that was run by two Huizhou merchants, one named Lutaichang, was very famous in Shanghai. But it suffered a setback and the two lost all of their money in three years. When Lutaichang's employees removed the shop's signboard, many bystanders claimed this signboard would never be hung again, but to everyone's surprise, the two Huizhou merchants returned and developed the fabric shop into a big name throughout the areas of Jiangsu and Zhejiang Provinces as well as Shanghai.

Anhui merchants also have a reputation for displaying high moral principles, benevolence, and humanity in their business activities. A Huizhou merchant named Wu Pengxiang once went to Sichuan to purchase pepper. When it was discovered that the pepper was poisonous, the seller begged him to keep it a secret. Instead, Wu bought the entire stock of 80,000 kg of the poisonous pepper and destroyed it before it could circulate in the market.

Many Anhui merchants were well known for showing good faith in their business transactions. A famous Huizhou ink maker named Hu Kaiwen developed a new waterproof ink cake. Attracted by the producer's reputation, a customer traveled a great distance to buy a bag of the ink cakes. On his return home, the bag of ink cakes fell into a river. As the ink cakes were expensive, the customer retrieved them but found that they had melted and were not waterproof after all. After being confronted by the customer, Hu apologized and offered a more expensive bag of ink cakes as compensation.

He then ordered the workshop to stop producing and selling the waterproof ink cakes, and offered customers a rebate in exchange for the faulty product and had those destroyed.

Anhui merchants had a strong sense of marketing. The above-mentioned Wu Pengxiang was in Hanyang engaged in the grain business when a severe famine struck the area, causing the price of rice to soar, multiplying several times in a single day. Thousands of dan of rice he had earlier purchased in Sichuan soon arrived, giving Wu the opportunity to make a fortune given the inflated market price. Instead, Wu sold the rice at a fair price which helped stabilize the market and pulled the population through a serious famine. At the same time, Wu earned a good reputation and was awarded special commendations from both the local and provincial governments. Wu's charitable act also turned out to be a very successful marketing strategy. Other examples of Huizhou craftiness in business include the story of Wang Yimei, a silk shop owner in Suzhou's Changmen area. Given the fierce competition, Wang offered 0.2 liang of silver to tailors in exchange for every Wang Yimei label they gave him, prompting tailors to always recommend Wang's cloth to their customers.

Perhaps the most famous Anhui merchant was Hu Xueyan. When he was 20 years old and working at a draft bank, Hu met a poor scholar named Wang Youling. Wang did not have enough money to go to the capital and take the imperial examinations, which was the only way for a poor scholar such as himself to be selected for a government position. Hu secretly lent Wang the money for the trip and was fired for this act. But once Wang secured a government position, he helped Hu become a rich businessman with interests in banking, pawnshops, herbal medicines, silk, and tea. It was also through Wang that Hu was given the role of bank official for the Zhejiang provincial government. In 1861, when government forces were battling the Taiping Army, Hu provided munitions and food in support of the government forces. Hu also had a close relationship with Zuo Zongtang, the governor of Zhejiang Province who was later promoted to senior governor in charge of Zhejiang and Fujian Provinces. Hu assisted Zuo in forming a joint army with the French to fight the Taiping Army. Hu also assisted in the establishment of the Shipbuilding Administration in Fujian. He was consequently assigned the task of procuring for the administration. On Zuo's recommendation, Hu was granted a second grade[13] official title and became a red-hat merchant.

Although Hu's government contacts contributed much to his success, his business acumen also played a crucial role. He put great effort into brand building as well as developing new products. He also implemented an incentive program to retain valued employees. In one particular business, when interviewing three candidates to fill the post of manager for Huqingyu Hall, a Chinese herbal medicine shop, Hu asked each candidate what they would do as manager. The first candidate promised the store would make an annual profit of 100,000 liang of silver in the first year of operation, and the second candidate said he would have the store running at a narrow profit the first two years and huge profit the third. The last candidate suggested that Hu invest all he could into building the best brand name possible and operate the store at a loss for three years, as they would only begin seeing profit after the brand was established. Hu was so impressed by the idea that the candidate was immediately hired and Hu proceeded to invest large sums in the R&D of the products, inviting the most esteemed herbal doctors from around the country to participate. He also began to give special bonuses to employees who contributed greatly to the enterprise, bonuses that were valid for a lifetime. In addition, Huqingyu Hall adopted two pensions for employees who had made special contributions—one was called "life pension," the other was called "afterlife pension." The former was a pension for retired or diseased employees. The latter was a survivor's pension granted to dead employees' families based on the worker's length of service.

Shanxi Merchants

Another major merchant group during the Ming and Qing Dynasties originated from China's north-western Shanxi Province. Similar to the high status of merchants in Huizhou, Shanxi people believed "he who excels in study can follow a commercial career."[14] They attached great importance to education and provided good studying conditions for their children. But this dedication to study was not to pursue a career as an official; instead, it was so the children could enhance their business careers. The Chang family were well-known wealthy merchants in the Yuci county of Shanxi. Brothers Chang Wangqi and Chang Wangda were the family's ninth generation descendants and were both excellent students. But instead of taking part in the imperial examinations to pursue an official career, they followed their father to run the family businesses in Zhangjiakou.[15] The two went on to achieve great success and the brands they created were among the most competitive among Shanxi merchants. In the Chang's 12th generation, there were two other descendants who so excelled in studies that both were enrolled in the Imperial College.[16] But they both elected to follow the path of their forefathers in business instead of officialdom.

Shanxi merchants shared another similarity with Anhui merchants—they were both excellent team workers. This was best exemplified in the two organizational mechanisms they created: the joint business and the merchant league. Joint businesses with friends or partners referred to an organizational model between two parties, one contributing capital and the other contributing effort. Such partnerships could reach a larger scale, as an investor could employ several partners to manage the business. This was a groundbreaking development in Chinese commerce. The merchant league was based on the joint business and was formed by relatives and fellow residents from the same township. Shanxi merchant leagues were established all over China and marked the functioning of these local groups.

Among the wide scope of businesses undertaken by Shanxi merchants, draft banking was the most outstanding. The first draft bank in China, Rishengchang, was founded by a Shanxi merchant family surnamed Li. The predecessor to Rishengchang was a dyestuff shop named Xiyucheng. In the late years of Emperor Jiaqing's (7th emperor of the Qing Dynasty) period, the development of commerce led to an increase in the inter-regional flow of cash. The traditional medium of payment by silver was both inconvenient and unsafe. The Xiyucheng dyestuff shop was the first to attempt draft transfers between Beijing and Shanxi, and when it proved effective, the shop began draft transfers as a new line of business. By the time of Emperor Daoguang's (8th emperor of the Qing Dynasty) period, the Xiyucheng dyestuff shop was formally renamed Rishengchang Draft Bank and became focused on draft transfers. Within a few years, Rishengchang opened over 100 branches across the country, covering all regions except north-eastern and south-western China. In its most prosperous period, Rishengchang's annual business volume reached 100 million liang of silver in draft transfers and 30 million liang of silver in loans.

Rishengchang's business model was quickly copied in the counties of Pingyao, Qixian, and Taigu of Shanxi, which formed into three major leagues playing a leading role in China's banking industry. Of the 51 major draft banks across the country, 43 were opened by Shanxi merchants. In 1907, Qixian county's first draft bank Heshengyuan initiated its international business by opening branches in the Japanese cities of Tokyo, Osaka, Yokohama, Kobe, and the Korean city of Sinuiju.

An important factor in the rise of Shanxi merchants was their links with the government. In the early years of the Ming Dynasty, its northern borders were troubled by remnants of the preceding Yuan Dynasty. To counter this problem, the Ming government built nine main garrison towns along the area where over 800,000 defense soldiers and 300,000 military horses were stationed. When supplying these towns proved problematic, Emperor Taizu (founding emperor of the Ming Dynasty) in 1370 implemented a policy whereby merchants who brought food to these towns were awarded "salt tickets."[17] Such tickets were used to buy salt which was sold for profit at specified areas. Due to proximity and their experience in the salt trade, Shanxi merchants were able to take full advantage of the policy, which enabled them to make their fortune and earn their reputation as good businessmen.

As early as the Ming Dynasty, Shanxi merchants were doing business with the Manchus[18] in spite of an imperial ban. After the establishment of the Qing Dynasty, eight Shanxi merchants were conferred the title of "imperial merchant." Included among them was the Fan family. In addition to their original trading business in the border areas, the Fan family was permitted to engage in salt trading in highly desirable areas due to population density and consumption volumes. During Emperor Yongzheng's (the 5th emperor of the Qing Dynasty) suppression of the Qinghai rebellion, the Fan family helped the imperial army by volunteering to transport military food supplies. In return, the Fan family was granted a special privilege—free trade with the nomadic peoples in the north-eastern regions.

Another well-known Shanxi merchant clan was the Qiao family. Gao Yu was the manager of the family's Dadetong company, and he was familiar with using the government to develop the business. He developed close ties with Zhao Erxun, a high-ranking official, and was able to reap excellent business deals from this relationship.

When Zhao was transferred to north-eastern China, Gao followed, and did so again when Zhao was moved to Beijing and Sichuan. The relationship was also beneficial to Zhao's political career as Dadetong's money gave him the support he needed.

The Shanxi merchants' success can be attributed to their business philosophy as well as their advanced and practical management skills. Qiao Zhiyong, founder of the Qiao family business, embraced a business philosophy that gave priority to credibility first, generosity second, and profits third. In one instance, the Qiao family purchased a large quantity of sesame oil in Baotou to sell in Shanxi, but a company clerk altered the oil for personal gain. When he was found out, Qiao Zhiyong demanded that notices be posted around the city to inform those who purchased the oil that it was contaminated and that they should return the oil for a full refund.

Shanxi merchants called their external business partners "Xiangyu," roughly translated as "business allies." When a Xiangyu was in trouble, Shanxi merchants often did their best to help, even at a cost to themselves. Dashengkui was the biggest Shanxi firm engaged in trade with Mongolia, meaning that it was a Xiangyu of Tianhengyu. When the latter faced bankruptcy, Dashengkui lent several tens of thousands of liang of silver to help Tianhengyu change the firm's name into Tianhengyong and survive the crisis. Later, when Dashengkui faced the same difficulty, Tianhengyong did the same.

Shanxi merchants were very careful in their selection of employees, who were mostly from their townships. The management was also promoted from within the company. Teenagers were often hired as apprentices, who were required to have people of wealth and prestige act as their guarantors. Promotions involved a training and evaluation process that lasted three to nine years. New apprentices were assigned to branches with the toughest working conditions, where they learned strict rules, professional skills, as well as moral and ethical standards. In the meantime, various methods were employed to test and evaluate the apprentices. As lodgings were provided within the shop, they were under constant scrutiny. Superiors could form a comprehensive and accurate appraisal of each apprentice with regard to skills and integrity. Based on such evaluations, those apprentices deemed worthy could rise through the ranks to become branch managers or even the general manager.

The internal management of Shanxi businesses placed the owner separate from the general manager, who was empowered to allocate capital, assign personnel, and operate the business. The general manager, who was based at the headquarters or head shop, was in charge of the management of various regional branches as well as the internal affairs of the head shop. Business development, capital employment, and the management of branches were delegated to branch managers. However, important decisions relating to organizational structure, capital allocation, the hiring and firing of personnel, as well as profit distribution were all made at the head shop. Branch managers reported to the owner and the general manager on their performance at the end of the year or accounting period.[19] Profit was not the sole measurement of performance. A more important criterion was the contribution a branch had made to the overall competitiveness of the head shop.

Shanxi merchants also came up with the concept of share holding. Shares in a business were divided into original shares and secondary shares according to the different types of profit distribution to which the holders were entitled. In terms of shareholder status, they were categorized into capital shares and labor shares. The original share was similar to registered capital and could claim stock bonuses but no dividends. The secondary share came from two sources: one was the owners' paid-in capital, and the other was the reinvestment of stock bonuses from shareholders, managers, and clerks with labor shares. It claimed dividends but no stock bonuses. Capital shares represent the owners' investment. Labor shares, also called labor contribution shares, were granted to the firm's key management staff such as the general manager and the assistant general manager. The entitlement to labor shares required no capital investment; they were for employees who had served the firm for a significant number of years after their apprenticeship. An employee's labor share usually amounted to 10% to 20% of one share initially.[20] Depending on the employee's capabilities and performance, it could gradually increase to a maximum of one share.

Labor shares were no different from capital shares in terms of profit distribution. The profit distribution on one share in one accounting period could be as much as 10,000 liang of silver. However, the two had fundamental differences. The holders of capital shares were the owners in the real sense as they had unlimited liabilities to the firm. Labor shares were a sort of incentive for employees aimed at giving the management team and the clerks a sense of ownership. Labor shares were entitled to profit distribution, but not liable to debt or loss, and they were not inheritable or transferable. But upon the death of the holder, his or her relatives could continue to get the dividend for a few additional years. However, if a manager or clerk was fired, the hard-won labor shares would be forfeited.

Ningbo Merchant Group

During the transitional period between the Qing Dynasty and the Republic of China, the Ningbo merchant group replaced the Anhui and Shanxi merchant groups as the most influential in China. Ningbo was also among the few areas in feudal China where merchants enjoyed a high level of social status. Two great Chinese philosophers and ideologists were from Ningbo; one was Wang Yangming of the Ming Dynasty. In his "New Commentaries on the Four Major Careers," Wang Yangming argued that there should not be any status difference among the careers of officials, farmers, craftsmen, and merchants because these were merely divisions of labor. The other great ideologist was Huang Zongxi of the late Ming and early Qing Dynasties. He pointed out that both industry and commerce were foundations of a nation. The Eastern Zhejiang[21] School of Thinking, of which Huang Zongxi was a leading scholar, believed that education should focus on what was useful to the real world. Huang emphasized the link between academic study and social realities, and these ideas were put into practice by the people of Ningbo. They taught their children practical skills that good merchants had such as calligraphy, letter writing, and abacus calculations instead of the "eight-part essay."[22]

Around the end of the Ming Dynasty and the start of the Qing Dynasty, Ningbo merchants gradually gained influence. In Emperor Chongzhen's period, Ningbo's herbal medicine merchants set up a Yinxian guild hall in Beijing, marking the establishment of the first Ningbo merchant organization. As with Anhui and Shanxi merchants, Ningbo merchants used guild halls as venues for gatherings, god worshipping ceremonies, and public activities. Through these activities, they kept close contact and helped solve each others' problems. In this way, they strengthened their competitive edge as a group over other merchants. There were two kinds of guild halls among Ningbo merchants. One was a friendship organization for those from the same native place. The other was a merchants' guild for those from the same native place, like the Yinxian guild hall. A very influential Ningbo merchant's guild of the time was the "Red Tailors' Guild," formed by Ningbo tailors in Shanghai. They specialized in making Western-style suits for foreigners, who were nicknamed "red haired," which is where the name Red Tailors' Guild came from.

It was said that the founder of the Red Tailors' Guild, Zhang Shangyi, was a survivor of a ship wreck while crossing the Hangzhou Gulf. He survived by grabbing onto a plank from the wreckage and floating for several days before landing on the shores of Yokohama in Japan. Finding himself in a foreign land, Zhang managed to make a living as a tailor mending the clothes of Russian sailors anchored at Yokohama. He gained a reputation for his hard work and became one of the best known tailors of Western suits. Years later, his son, Zhang Yousong, returned to Shanghai and established China's first Western suit tailor shop—Fuchang Western Suit Tailor Shop. He eventually opened shops across the country, all the while teaching his hometown folks tailoring skills. For a long period, all of the best tailors in Shanghai's busiest commercial street were run by Ningbo merchants. They were responsible for many firsts in Chinese contemporary clothing. They made the first Western-styled suit, the first Sun Yat-sen suit,[23] and even wrote China's first book on suit tailoring methods. Even after 1949, the clothes worn by the founders of the People's Republic of China, including Mao Zedong, were almost all made by Ningbo tailors.

Without the close connection with government officials that Anhui and Shanxi merchants had, Ningbo merchants were typically "commoner-merchants." The first important phase for Ningbo merchants was during the reigns of the 6th and 7th emperors of the Qing Dynasty, Emperor Qianlong and Emperor Jiaqing, when the maritime trade of Ningbo merchants grew rapidly. They traveled further afield beyond the Yangtze River and they replaced Fujian merchants as the main copper dealers with the Japanese.

The second important phase for Ningbo merchants was after the Opium War.[24] With their experience in overseas transactions, they eagerly entered the emerging foreign trade market. They became compradors[25] and foreign trade dealers, marking the emergence of a new type of merchant in China. Their business sphere had transcended the traditional commodity exchange typical of the small-scale peasant economy. It was international trade based on the exchange of the domestic agricultural products for Western industrial products. Since the 1890s the number of Ningbo compradors had exceeded those from Guangdong and they became the largest comprador group in Shanghai. Later, their presence was extended to Tianjin and Hankou. Ningbo traders, meanwhile, ventured into modern industrial trade in such things as metal, coloring agents, machinery, and hardware manufacturing. And although these sectors were almost a monopoly of Ningbo merchants, they depended heavily on Westerners. Many of them were employed by trading companies, banks, or shipping companies run by Western merchants, helping them sell Western merchandise.

The mid to late 19th century was the third important phase for Ningbo merchants. They invested their profits into emerging industries such as shipping, finance, and manufacturing. This represented a strong national and industrial capital. Some examples are:

- In 1854, three Ningbo merchants Fei Lunzhi, Li Yeting, and Sheng Zhiguan bought from Britain the first commercial ship in China. The ship cost 70,000 liang of silver and was named "Baoshun." They later established the Qingcheng Shipping Company.
- In 1862, Ningbo merchant Ye Chengzhong opened a foreign hardware store in Shanghai. It was the first Chinese-owned hardware store in Shanghai. Ye's business was later expanded all across the country, with a total of 38 branches and 108 joint branches. He was nicknamed the "Hardware King."
- In 1896, Ningbo merchant Bao Xianchang, with brother Bao Xianen and brother-in-law Xia Ruifang, established the Commercial Press. It grew to be the biggest publishing house in contemporary China.
- In 1897, Ningbo merchants Yan Xinhou, Ye Chengzhong, and Zhu Baosan established the first Chinese bank—the Commercial Bank of China.
- In 1912, Ningbo merchant Fang Yexian founded the Consumer Chemicals Firm in Shanghai. It was the first

producer of consumer chemicals in China. The products included tooth powder, toothpaste, mosquito repellent incense, and soap. Fang Yexian was regarded as the founder of consumer chemicals in China.

- In 1915, Ningbo merchant Yu Qiaqing founded Sanbei Shipping Group. It was China's biggest commercial shipping group at the time. Its gross annual tonnage reached 91,000 tons, which was one-seventh of the total handled by Chinese-run shipping companies.
- In 1923, Ningbo merchant Zhou Xiangsheng founded the Xiangsheng Taxi Company in Shanghai. By 1937, with 22 branches and 230 taxis, it had become the biggest taxi company in Shanghai.
- Ningbo merchant Liu Hongsheng made his fortune in coal and was nicknamed the "Coal King." In 1930, he founded the Greater China Match Company. It was the biggest match plant in China at the time, producing one-fourth of the total national output. Liu thus earned another nickname—"Match King."

The fourth important phase for Ningbo merchants was during the several decades following the 1940s and 1950s. A number of Ningbo merchants moved overseas during this period; most chose to go to Hong Kong, where some of them succeeded in establishing international business empires. When Ningbo merchant Bao Yugang moved to Hong Kong in early 1949, he was initially in the trading business. In 1955, starting with a second-hand cargo ship, Bao entered the maritime shipping market. After over 20 years, he built up the Global Shipping Bloc. By the end of the 1970s, the bloc owned more than 200 large and super-large carriers with a total tonnage of over 20 million tons, which was more than the overall tonnage of the national cargo fleet of the United States or the former Soviet Union. In the 1980s, Bao expanded his business sphere by purchasing shares of the British-funded Wharf Holdings and Wheelock Marden and investing in Cathay Pacific and Dragon Airlines. His business empire covered shipping, real estate, hotels, communications, airlines, warehousing, wharfs, and trade.

Another Ningbo merchant Run Run Shaw and his brother founded the Unique Film Company in Shanghai. They went to Singapore in 1926 to open up its film market and founded Shaw

Brothers film company. When Hong Kong's economy started to gain momentum, Shaw went there in 1958 and founded Shaw Brothers (Hong Kong) Limited. After the 1960s, Shaw Brothers produced more than 1,000 films and won scores of film awards such as the Taiwan Golden Horse Awards and Hong Kong Film Awards. In the 1970s, Shaw Brothers entered the television industry. In 1980, as the biggest individual shareholder, Shaw was elected chairman of the board of directors of Hong Kong Television Broadcasts (TVB). He later focused on the management of the subsidiary Pearl Channel and Jade Channel. Audience ratings for these two channels have long been number one in Hong Kong.

Chinese Merchants in South East Asia

The contributions of Chinese merchants to the development of capitalism was not limited to China; they also played an important role in South East Asia. The Chinese tended to emigrate for four main reasons: political exile; social and natural disasters such as flood and war; seeking money-making opportunities; and study. A great majority of Chinese immigrated to take part in economic activities, especially to South East Asian countries.

Chinese immigration to other Asian countries dates back to the Han Dynasty, but it was not until the most prosperous period of the Tang Dynasty (618 AD to 907 AD) that immigration accelerated. Rapid development in ship building and navigation techniques, combined with a strong national government, allowed for such movement, leading to numerous trade links with many Asian countries. In the following 700 to 800 years until the middle of the Ming Dynasty, Chinese merchants settled and built up their economic strength in these countries.

Large-scale immigration to South East Asia took place from the second half of the 16th century to the Opium War in 1840. It was during this period that Western colonialists in Asia began developing the economies, leading to a strong demand for workers. Many of these workers came from Fujian and Guangdong Provinces. The total number of Chinese immigrants in Asia at this time reached one million.

While many Chinese merchants were employed overseas as contract workers, a number of them turned to running their own businesses once their contracts ended. Seeing the huge demand created by the monopolistic British firms, some Chinese merchants established plants to process raw materials; others acted as intermediaries in trade. Chinese banks and trade associations in the 19th century also facilitated the movement of capital. Despite all these activities, the Chinese played a relatively minor role compared to that of the Western colonial powers.

One by one, from the end of World War II to the 1960s, South East Asian countries began to gain independence, and the stronghold colonial powers had in these economies was weakened, opening opportunities for domestic capital growth. Countries implemented an "import substitution" strategy by raising tariffs, restricting imports, and overvaluing exchange rates. Many Chinese merchants seized on these opportunities and shifted their businesses from commerce and trade to industrial enterprises. It was during this period that the Lin family in Indonesia changed its Salim Group from a clove trading company to a flour and textile producer. And in Malaysia, the Kuok Brothers Sdn Bhd was changed from a sugar and flour trading company to a flour and textile producer. It was not until the 1970s that South East Asian countries adopted an "export-oriented" strategy by lowering tariffs, rewarding exports, and encouraging foreign investment. A number of Chinese merchants set up joint ventures with foreign investors to process and assemble industrial products and intermediary products for the international market. One such example was the Tan Chong Group in Malaysia that shifted from being a dealer and assembler for Japanese auto companies to the manufacturing of auto parts for the European and North American markets. Tan Chong has since become the largest manufacturer and exporter of auto parts in Malaysia.

During this period, the concept of stocks was introduced to South East Asian countries and stock markets were established. A number of Chinese-owned enterprises were listed on the stock markets and began investing in the shares of other companies in a big way, thereby expanding their spheres of business. For example, since the 1970s, the Salim Group began acquiring and merging flour mills, cement plants, automobile factories, and banks. It gradually became a major player in the processing and distribution of flour, cement producing, automobile manufacturing, and financing in Indonesia, and is one of the largest Chinese-owned enterprises in that country. Singapore's Chinese-owned United Overseas Bank became the biggest privately owned banking group in the city state through acquiring four local banks.

In the 1980s, South East Asian countries adopted a series of favorable policies to promote the development of basic industries and many large industrial and chemical projects were initiated. A number of large groups expanded during this period, especially those in the steel industry, such as the Lion Group of Malaysia, and Thailand's Sahaviriya Mill Plate and SSP Group.

In *Forbes'* 2005 Rich List of the top 40 East Asian billionaires, about 30 were of Chinese origin and nine of the top 10 were Chinese. On top of the list was chairman of Kuok Brothers Sdn Bhd, Robert Kuok Hock Nien. Kuok's father was a native of Fujian who went to Malaysia in 1909 and started his business from scratch. Soon after Kuok graduated from Singapore's Raffles College in 1948 he founded a shipping company.

In 1957, when Malaysia gained independence from its English colonial ruler, Kuok realized that the withdrawal of the British would inevitably leave a vacuum in the domestic consumer market. He joined forces with the government to establish the first Malaysian sugar refinery in 1959, buying raw sugar from Thailand, processing it, and distributing it all over the country. In a few years, Kuok controlled Malaysia's sugar industry. In 1968, Kuok leased 140,000 acres of land from the government to grow sugarcane and build refineries. His efforts enabled Malaysia to become self-sufficient with regard to sugar. In 1970, he purchased a large amount of crude sugar before sugar prices rose in the global market, and invested heavily in the sugar futures market. The Kuok Brothers' share of the domestic sugar market reached 80%. Their engagement in the multilateral trade of sugar enabled them to control a total of 1.5 million tons of sugar annually, which was 10% of the international market.

Kuok entered the hotel industry in 1971 when he invested 100 million ringgit to build the first Shangri-La Hotel in Singapore. He gradually expanded the brand into Malaysia, Thailand, Hong Kong, Fiji, Seoul, the Philippines, and mainland China, making the Shangri-La Hotels and Resorts one of the top five-star hotel brands in the world. Kuok implemented another strategic move during this period. In January 1974, he founded Kerry Group in Hong Kong for futures trading. A few years later, the Hong Kong government decided to develop the reclaimed eastern part of Tsimshatsui and offered plots for auction. Seizing upon the opportunity, Kuok forged deals with Hong Kong real estate developers and bought several sites, building a Shangri-La Hotel on one of them. The hotel was a great success. Shortly after it opened, it was ranked third-best hotel in the world by Hong Kong magazines.

In the early 1980s, the Sino–British Joint Declaration was signed, stipulating the return of Hong Kong to China in 1997. Confident in Hong Kong's future, Kuok increased his real estate investments in Hong Kong and purchased a site in Tuen Mun, where he built a yacht club and luxury residences. In 1984, Kuok invested HK$400 million to establish the Aberdeen Marina Club, and in 1988 he invested another HK$1.37 billion toward the acquisition of Branksome Crest, Century Tower, and May Tower.

In the 1990s, Kuok extended its business sphere into media, film, and television. The Kerry Group purchased the English-language newspaper the *South China Morning Post*, and invested in Television Broadcast Limited (TVB) and became one of its major shareholders.

The Cultural Revolution

In the early stages in the establishment of the People's Republic of China, Chairman Mao Zedong proposed that capitalism should be allowed "an extensive development" in China. However, with the launch of the so-called "Three Antis" campaign at the end of 1951, the fate of China's private economy began to change.

The anti-corruption-focused "Three Antis" campaign was aimed against corruption within the Communist Party. It exposed those who accepted bribes as well as those who offered them. Among them was a private Shanghai pharmacy owner who offered bribes to 65 cadres in 25 government agencies. Categorized as RMB 19,000 in "communications fees" in his accounting records, the bribes brought in RMB 110,000 worth of orders from these government agencies. Other practices were also revealed, such as the use of inferior material in the supply of equipment for military fighting in the Korean War. The campaign was quickly followed by the "Five Antis" targeted against bribery, tax evasion, theft of state property, cheating on government contracts, and stealing state economic information. This second campaign was not supported by legal means, thus leading to confusion, and many private businessmen were unjustly accused. Among them was shipping magnate Lu Zuofu.

Lu Zuofu was a native of Sichuan Province. In 1926 he started from scratch and founded Minsheng Company. He opened shipping lines on the Jialing River and proposed a management philosophy of "All for Customers." Every Minsheng employee, from manager to sailor, was somewhat engaged in serving their customers. They offered Minsheng customers a full and considerate service. Lu himself often boarded a ship to serve passengers. Minsheng made a profit of over RMB 20,000 in the first year of operation. In 1929, Lu was appointed the director of Chuanjiang[26] Water Transport Administration. Competition was fierce at the time; foreign shipping companies undercut domestic players putting many domestic companies on the verge of bankruptcy. As director of the water administration, Lu Zuofu implemented regulations requiring foreign ships destined for Chongqing to go through customs clearance at the Chuanjiang administration. He also encouraged the integration of the small companies into one big company, and from 1930 Minsheng began merging and acquiring domestic shipping companies. In less than a year, seven companies successfully merged with Minsheng, and by 1935 Minsheng had beaten its American and British competitors. The company purchased another 11 vessels, increasing its shipping fleet to 42 ships with a total capacity of 16,884 tons. Minsheng's market share of Chuanjiang waterway transport reached 61%.

When the anti-Japanese war was over, Lu Zuofu moved the focus of his shipping lines on the Yangtze River to Shanghai. Radiating from Shanghai were new routes to Taiwan, Hong Kong, Lianyungang, Qingdao, Tianjin, and Yingkou. Minsheng opened operations in Taiwan, Guangzhou, and Hong Kong, and by 1949 Minsheng's shipping fleet increased to 150 ships, with a total capacity of 72,000 tons. In 1950, Lu Zuofu left Hong Kong and returned to Beijing.

In February 1952, at a meeting of the "Five Antis" campaign, Lu's office boy accused Lu of bribery. The alleged bribery occurred during a Minsheng board meeting, when Lu treated holders of public shares (government officials appointed to enterprises of joint state–private ownership) to dinner and a performance of Beijing Opera. He also gave them each a woolen overcoat as a present. Lu was already under tremendous pressure as a Minsheng vessel had hit a rock and sunk several days earlier. The incident was rumored to have been an act of sabotage by Kuomintang agents, and this had caused intense tensions within the company. After he was accused of bribery, Lu could withstand the pressure no longer and committed suicide three days later.

According to the findings and evaluations of the "Five Antis" campaign, only 10% to 15% of private enterprises were classified as "law abiding," 50% to 60% as "basically law abiding," 25% to 30% as "semi-law abiding," 4% as "serious lawbreaking," and 1% as "completely lawbreaking." The result led to the central government's change of policies toward private enterprises.

At the end of 1953, the central government set to transform private enterprises. Its first step was to take control of main materials including coal, metal, chemicals, and textiles, and put the supply of raw materials under state control, thereby cutting supply to private enterprises. Meanwhile, the central government implemented a policy that put the purchase and sale of main agricultural products such as grain, edible oil, and cotton completely under state control, implementing a state monopoly. This measure forced private enterprises out of the distribution of these agricultural products. Secondly, private-owned wholesalers, retailers, and traders were also transformed—state-owned commercial entities replaced private-owned wholesalers; private-owned retailers were transformed into dealers or outlets of state-owned commerce; and private export and import traders were transformed into two forms of ownership, namely ownership on a commission basis and joint state–private ownership.

In September 1954, the state policy on "joint state–private ownership" was promulgated. Through joint state–private ownership, the state invested in and appointed cadres to the formerly private enterprises. The state investment took the form of public shares and the state-appointed cadres were the representatives of the public shares. In 1955, for individual private enterprises to be transformed into joint state–private ownership the state invested RMB 1,273 for every RMB 10,000 of private assets and appointed one representative for every 63 employees. For an industry to be transformed as a whole into joint state–private ownership, the state invested only RMB 86 for every RMB 10,000 worth of private assets, and appointed one representative for every 160 employees. The control of a joint state–private ownership enterprise was not determined by the size of investment; instead, the representatives of the public shares and workers controlled the enterprise. The original enterprise owners were relegated to a subordinate role. Enterprises didn't operate to make a profit, but instead to meet state requirements by producing and managing assets according to state plans. By 1956, when the transformation into joint state–private ownership was completed, more than 800,000 private businessmen lost their ownership, leaving very few private-owned enterprises in China.

At the early founding period of the People's Republic of China, there were over 50 million self-employed craftsmen. They underwent a transformation that began with a cooperative model whereby small cooperative groups were formed on a voluntary basis, processing products for sale at state-owned enterprises or "supply and marketing cooperatives." By the end of 1955, the state sought to reform this model and implemented a series of new policies. All craftsmen were required to join handicraft cooperatives, which was a form of collective ownership. By June 1956, most craftsmen had joined cooperatives, and only 10% were self-employed.

In 1949 there were about 6.5 million small private shops (or mom-and-pop stores). Initially, their transformation took the following forms: turned into dealers or outlets for state-owned commerce; united purchase with but separate sale from state-owned commerce, each party assuming independent responsibility for its own profits or losses; and united purchase and sale with the state-owned commerce, the two parties sharing profits and losses. In 1956, joint state–private ownership reform was also carried out among small private shops. By the end of the year, only 14.9% of them remained untransformed, most of which were in remote areas or were not in regular operation.

After three years of transformation, China's private economy in 1956 was on its last gasps. The Cultural Revolution dealt private businesses a final blow and almost wiped it out. In September 1966, the state government promulgated national policies: all joint state–private owned enterprises were to be transformed into state-owned enterprises. All big joint state–private owned shops were to be transformed into state-owned shops. All small private-owned shops that had not been transformed into joint state-owned ownership were to be transformed into outlets of state-owned shops. From 1968 to 1970, the central government enforced a series of regulations in which private commercial businesses were defined as "illegal profiteering and speculation" and "anti-revolutionary economic activities," and were strictly forbidden. It was also reiterated that except for the state-owned commercial sector, no organization or individual was permitted to engage in commercial activities. In the meantime, no organization was allowed to purchase commodities at marketplaces, rural communes, or from production teams. During the Cultural Revolution, the business of self-employed craftsmen such as shoe mending, bicycle repairing, tailoring, and peddling was also inhibited. In 1973, individual self-employed craftsmen represented only 0.8% of employment in the industrial sector. In the commercial sector, only 0.2% of sales were from the individual self-employed craftsmen.

Meanwhile, farmers were required to contribute their crops to the commune without compensation. Household animal husbandry, gathering, weaving and carpentry, ironsmith and masonry were also restricted. In some regions, every household was permitted to breed only one pig and one chicken per member of the household. Breeding sows were forbidden in some areas to control the number of pigs. Household animal husbandry was for self-sufficiency, not for sale in the marketplace. Selling eggs was also considered "illegal profiteering and speculation." In a county of Liaoning Province, mat weaving was a traditional sideline for farmers. Before the Cultural Revolution, the region's annual output of mats reached over 160,000. Following the restrictions, the output in 1976 fell to 5,000.

In addition to the broad overview of changes to China's private economy, a more direct impression can be obtained from the state profit distribution policies on private enterprises:

- According to the Temporary Regulations on Private Enterprises of 1950, after taxation and 10% public reserve funds, at least 60% of private enterprises' profit were retained by private owners.
- In 1953, the profit distribution policy shifted to: 34.5% for taxation, 15% for employee welfare, 30% for public reserve funds, 20.5% for private owners.
- After the joint state–private ownership reforms in 1956, the profit distribution policy was changed to a fixed interest. Private owners were entitled to a fixed interest equal to 5% of the value of their original capital goods.

- During the Cultural Revolution, with the transformation of all private enterprises into state-owned ones, the 5% fixed interest for the private owners was cancelled.

"The class struggle-centered" Cultural Revolution in fact caused overall political, social, and economic chaos in China. The whole national economy was on the verge of collapse. As an old Chinese saying goes, "When the nest is overturned, no egg stays unbroken."

The Period of Reform and Opening-up

As indicated in the last chapter, the destiny of China's private economy was determined by government policy. Its revival was fittingly due to government policies toward reform and opening up, beginning in 1976. This process could be divided into three phases:

1. The removal of the prohibition on private economy
2. Another blow for private economy
3. The rapid development of private economy

The Removal of the Prohibition on Private Economy

At the end of 1978, the third plenary session of the 11th National Congress of the Chinese Communist Party (CCP) made a landmark decision to revive and speed up the development of agriculture, regarded as the foundation of the national economy, in an effort to rebuild the depressed economy. As part of this policy, the prohibition against private economic activities on farms—such as the cultivation of private fields, poultry, picking, weaving as well as marketplace trading—was removed. From the autumn of 1980 to the end of 1982, the household contracting system had been universally adopted in rural China. Household contracting refers to contracting output quota of agriculture and sideline economic activities to each rural household, and the rural household's income was linked to the output. As a result of the household contracting system, farmers received sufficient income and became owners of private properties, including private residences, bank savings, and means of production. In the meantime, the household contracting system stimulated entrepreneurship among those inclined in rural areas, thus laying the foundation for rapid development of township and village enterprises (TVEs)[27] after 1984.

In urban areas, a large number of "educated urban youth," who were dispatched to work on farms, returned to the cities after the Cultural Revolution. Finding employment for them was an urgent matter. In addressing this issue, the state government from 1979 to 1983 implemented a series of policies to legalize the existence and encourage the development of craftsmen and individual businesses.

In 1980, the government decided to establish four Special Economic Zones (SEZs) in the cities of Shenzhen, Zhuhai, Shantou, and Xiamen, as an "experimental field" to test economic reforms. The SEZs attracted tens of thousands of ambitious young people, many of whom started from scratch and built successful enterprises.

The 12th National Congress of the CCP held in October 1984 made the decision to carry out economic reform and to build a market economy. In the meantime, it admitted the legal status of individual businesses and their important supplementary role in promoting economic development and increasing employment.

Among our 20 featured entrepreneurs, two took their first steps toward entrepreneurship following these decisions. In 1985, Lu Wenlong from Zhejiang set to pursue his dreams of becoming a millionaire by contracting the management of a TVE. In 1986, a 16-year-old Liu Qiongying rented a nine-meter storefront and opened a shoe shop, laying the foundation for her multi-million-dollar company, Aiminger Leather Products.

The constitutional amendment passed in April 1988 stated explicitly: the state permits the private economy to exist and develop; the state protects the lawful rights and interests of the private economy. In the same year, the state government promulgated Provisional Regulations on Private-Owned Enterprises and Provisional Regulations on the Income Tax of Private-Owned Enterprises. All these state laws and regulations affirmed the legal status of the private sector.

It was also in 1988 that the central government named Hainan as the fifth SEZ, leading to a deluge of youth to the island, each seeking their fortune. Against this background, one of our featured entrepreneurs quit his job at an SOE and went to Hainan, where he went on to establish Hainan Zhongxin Chemical.

Private Economy Suffers Another Setback

From 1989 to 1991, a nationwide ideological debate on "capitalism versus socialism" halted the development of the private economy in

China. Some began questioning whether the household contracting system, the individual businesses, the TVEs and such would turn China into a capitalist state. Many individual and private business owners closed their operations, fearful of a re-emergence of the Cultural Revolution.

Statistics show that by the second half of 1989, the number of registered individual businesses dropped to 12.34 million, with total employment in individual businesses reduced to 19.44 million, down respectively by 15% and 15.7% from the previous year. In 1988, there were a total of two million private enterprises in China, but at the end of 1989 the number was reduced to 906,000. It saw little increase in 1990, and in 1991 it increased to one million, a slight increase from the previous year.

The Rapid Development of Private Economy

In 1990, the state government selected Pudong New District in Shanghai as the next destination for opening up, which opened the floodgate for fortune hunters. Half of our 20 entrepreneurs got their start in Shanghai. Five of them chose Shanghai because of the state's favorable policies in Pudong.

In early 1992, Deng Xiaoping visited southern China and delivered the famous South China Speeches.[28] When the 14th National Congress of the CCP was held in October later that year, it decided to speed up economic development and accelerate the pace of reform and opening up. The South China Speeches and the resolution of the 14th National Congress of the CCP dispelled the cloud of uncertainty cast upon individual and private business ownership. At the same time, many government officials and intellectuals quit their jobs and became engaged in private businesses. This phenomenon was called "jumping into the sea." According to statistics from the State Ministry of Personnel, a total of 120,000 government employees quit and entered private enterprises. The number of those who kept their jobs and became engaged in commercial activities reached 10 million. Among our sampled entrepreneurs, two of them quit their government jobs and "jumped into the sea."

In this way, China's private economy quickly climbed out of its low ebb. In 1993, the number of POEs increased to 2.37 million and their registered capital reached RMB 240 billion between 1994 and 1995, 20 times the total from 1989 to 1990. Among our sampled entrepreneurs, a quarter of them started their enterprises between 1994 and 1995.

In 1997, at the 15th National Congress of the CCP, the private economy was called an "important component" of the national economy. Compared with the previous official definition of private economy as a supplement to the state economy, the status of the private sector was greatly strengthened. It resulted in further acceleration of the development of China's private economy. Among our 20 sampled entrepreneurs, five of them started their enterprises in 1997.

Wenzhou

The role of the people of Wenzhou in the development of China's private economy during this period is as important as that of Anhui, Shanxi, and Ningbo merchants. Since the end of the 1970s and the beginning of 1980s, the number of household workshops grew quickly in Wenzhou. By the mid-1980s, there were a total of 300,000 household workshops in Wenzhou engaged in the production of small goods; they accounted for 70% of the value of industrial output. It was called the "Wenzhou model."

One of our subjects, Michael Ma, is from Wenzhou and his business model is fairly typical. "At that time, it was not about building a long-term sustainable enterprise, it was about making money. Wherever we could make money, we would do it. I could be engaged in three to five different businesses at the same time," he says. As for the special characteristics of a Wenzhou business person, Michael notes that people from Wenzhou were no smarter than those from any other place, the only difference is that they had an early start and tended to experiment. He gives two examples of such experiments, which follow.

The township of Longgang in Wenzhou was well known at the time for the local government's achievements in promoting economic and political reforms. Because it was a newly established town, few people wanted to move there. To encourage immigration, the local government began selling land at low prices. When this tactic proved ineffective, the government decided to "allocate" the land to government employees at a very low price. These two acts may not seem dramatic today, but in 1984 it was unheard of and highly innovative. As land prices increased, so too did Longgang's population.[29] Another example of such experimental thinking is a directive issued by the

Wenzhou government in the early 1990s. Government employees were encouraged to quit their jobs and "jump into the sea" of private business in exchange for cash. Michael's wife took advantage of this policy and received RMB 40,000 in cash. A government employee's average monthly salary at the time was only RMB 300 to RMB 400.

It is obvious that the robust growth of the private economy in Wenzhou was to a great extent shaped by the local government's policy support.

Notes

1. In Chinese phonetics, the name is written as Zhang Qian.
2. From the 3rd century BC to the 8th century BC, the middle Asian area was called the Western Regions.
3. Nomadic pastoral people of Central Asia. The Xiongnu at the end of the 3rd century BC formed a great tribal league that dominated much of Central Asia for more than 500 years. Their threat to the northern Chinese frontier throughout this period led to China's eventual conquest of northern Korea and southern Manchuria during the Han Dynasty.
4. A unit in the Chinese weight system. Twenty liang is about one kilogram.
5. A region in the modern Huangshan City of Anhui Province. Most of the Anhui merchants were from this area.
6. In Chinese "Cao" (漕) means water transport.
7. Chinese unit of dry measure, equalling 100 liters.
8. The sixteenth and last emperor of the Ming Dynasty. His reign was between 1627 and 1644.
9. An important political and economic center at that time. The center of the salt trade in the Huaihe River area.
10. A major river in Jiangsu Province.
11. Government officials in the Ming and Qing Dynasty wore hats with some red ornaments on top. Red-hat merchants refer to those merchants who hold honorary official titles in the government.
12. "Wen" is a unit in the ancient Chinese monetary system. At the early days of Emperor Daoguang's period, one liang of silver equaled 1,000 wen.
13. There were nine grades in the government hierarchy of the Qing Dynasty. The second grade was equal to the governor of a province.
14. This is derived from a Confucian slogan for education: "He who excels in study can follow an official career."
15. A city in Hebei Province, north-east of Shanxi.
16. The highest educational administration of the time. Its students were granted official titles upon graduation without taking the imperial examination.
17. The use of salt tickets can be dated back to the Song Dynasty (960–1279). Merchants engaged in salt trade must have salt tickets issued by the government. Usually one must pay in money or kind to get them. It's a government mechanism for the state monopoly of the salt trade.

18. The native people of Manchuria, who ruled China during the Qing dynasty.
19. One accounting period usually lasted three to five years.
20. The number of original shares of a firm was usually from 10 to 15.
21. Ningbo is located on the coastline of the eastern part of Zhejiang Province.
22. The style of writing that was used in the imperial examinations during the Ming and the Qing Dynasties. It was generally believed to be obsolete and useless except for the imperial examinations.
23. Sun Yat-sen (*Sun Zhongshan*) (1866–1925), the Provisional President of the new Chinese Republic proclaimed in 1911, is credited with the modernization of Chinese men's dress. It is said that he instructed Huang Longsheng, a Western-style tailor from Ningbo, to design a suit based on one commonly worn by Chinese men in Japan and south-east Asia.
24. The two wars fought around the middle of the 19th century (1840–1843 and 1856–1860 respectively) between China and Britain, also called the Anglo-Chinese Wars. In the second war, France fought alongside Britain. Britain was smuggling opium from British India into China, and when China attempted to enforce her laws against the trade, the conflict erupted. China succumbed in both wars and was forced to tolerate the opium trade and sign unequal treaties opening several ports to foreign trade and yielding Hong Kong to Britain. Several countries followed Britain and forced unequal terms of trade onto China.
25. A native-born agent in China and certain other Asian countries formerly employed by a foreign business to serve as a collaborator or an intermediary in commercial transactions.
26. In Chinese, Chuanjiang means "rivers in Sichuan." Besides Yangzi River, other major rivers in Sichuan include Jialing River and Min River.
27. Enterprises operated by rural townships and villages, a group of farmers, or individuals in the rural areas of China. At the beginning, most TVEs were of the townships and villages' collective ownership. Most of them have gradually transformed to individual ownership.
28. In January 1992, Deng Xiaoping made an inspection tour to South China and delivered a series of speeches to promote the further opening up and deepening reform of China. The speeches are collectively called the South China Speeches.
29. By the end of 2006, Longgang's population had reached 200,000.

CHAPTER

Three Stories

The Story of Michael Ma

Breaking Away from the State-Owned Structure

In the mid-1980s, over 300,000 rural residents in Wenzhou were engaged in the production of small wares in household workshops. This led to a rapid economic restructuring and urbanization of Wenzhou. The city became renowned in China for the so-called "Wenzhou model."

As a student in Wenzhou, Michael Ma narrowly failed the highly competitive national college entrance exam, where only 3% of applicants are accepted. In 1980, at 18 years old, he began working at a local branch of the People's Bank of China (PBC), and was transferred to a local branch of the Industrial and Commercial Bank of China (ICBC) when it was established at the end of 1983. And in 1987, he left the bank to vie for the post of Secretary of the Chinese Communist Youth League, which the Longgang government opened for public election.

There were over 1,000 candidates in the first round, but by the fourth round, Michael was elected. For most candidates, winning a government post meant obtaining urban resident status, which was more important than the post itself. Michael, on the other hand, wanted the job because he thought it would offer him freedom and less pressure. To his disappointment, however, the government job was far from what he expected, and after only four years, he decided to quit. The decision met with strong opposition from his parents, who both worked at government institutions. He told them the following:

> *If I stay, I'd have to be both extremely capable and lucky to reach the top post—party secretary of the county [the leader of the local government]—by the time I'm 50. And even if this comes true, what's the big deal? I'd get a car—a Volkswagen Santana—which would be taken back when I retired at 60. But if I could make enough money, I would buy my own car and have it for a lifetime. You might be worried about my failing and ending up with nothing. If that's the case, I'll give you all the money I've saved so far. Then if I fail, I could always come back to you.*

Profit-Oriented Business Operations

In addition to his dim view on a political career, Michael had another reason for leaving the government post. In 1984, he had opened a small workshop while working at the bank. He bought a machine and hired workers to produce small wares such as plastic wares, printing, and photoengraving products. His main product line was packaging, such as ice-cream boxes and paper cups. Like most household workshops in Wenzhou, its business model was quite simple: production began upon receipt of the customer's down-payment; and the balance was paid once delivery had been made and the customer had examined the goods.

Michael describes an incident during the early days of the workshop. He had received an order from a Shanghai soap manufacturer for soap packages. After the customer failed to pick up the product, Michael took the packages to Shanghai and tried to find the customer. The only contact information he had was a telephone number, and when he called it he discovered that the customer was not the manufacturer but a middleman. After additional searching, he found the manufacturer, delivered the goods, and received payment. More importantly, he established direct contact with the manufacturer.

The business prospered, and he was soon making several thousand RMB a month, a far cry from the RMB 100 he made at the bank and the RMB 200 to RMB 300 salary he received from the government. This huge disparity made him determined to quit his job and devote his time to the workshop when it expanded operations in 1991. Since he already had business contacts in Shanghai, he decided to pursue greater opportunities there and rented a warehouse in the outskirts of the city. But business was hampered by a prevalent problem at the time, failure of prompt payment by his customers. He went so far as to help customers sell their products so he could get paid.

In 1992, Michael returned to Wenzhou and registered a limited liability company with RMB 2 million capital. He also invested in a biscuit factory, and a packaging factory where he was chairman but was not involved in their operations. At that time, China's biscuit industry was small with few product lines. At the end of the 1980s and the beginning of the 1990s, investors from Hong Kong, Macau, and Taiwan built over 30 biscuit factories around the Pearl River Delta area. Their advanced technology and biscuit recipes enabled them to capture more than half of the market in China. Seeing this success, many local enterprises emerged and copied their business models.

The biscuit business proved a difficult one. Profit margins were narrow, and despite investing RMB 6 million into the factory, Michael decided to close it down in 1996 after suffering losses of RMB 1 million. Reflecting on the failure, Michael summarized two factors: his lack of understanding of the biscuit industry and the consequent lack of core competence; and to make any profit, a factory that cannot achieve economies of scale (its daily output was 20 tons) should be run by hardworking and thrifty people like his parents.

A reason why Michael maintained the failing business for so long was because Wenzhou people were highly concerned about their credit. Wenzhou was one place in China where private financing played a very active role in business. If Michael had closed his factory within the first year or two, his credit would have been affected. Few would have trusted him and it would be very difficult for him to obtain any private financing later on. Because of this, Michael used the money he had made from the packaging factory to maintain the biscuit factory until its closure.

In 1993, Michael invested in real estate in a cooperative initiative with the Shanghai municipal government. He bought a large area of land in a development zone in the suburbs of Shanghai with an eye to selling pieces of it for profit. But the state government's macro-control measures that year severely impacted the real estate sector and there were few buyers. Michael soon saw the interest rates on his bank loans rise to 22% between 1993 and 1995. Banks in Wenzhou were experimenting with interest rates, which were set by the market and not the banks themselves. Debtors were able to negotiate interest rates with banks, but Michael's main concern was losing the land due to the government's failure to develop the zone. So he lowered his prices and sold most of his land. After this experience, Michael bought a number of apartments in Wenzhou and Shanghai, and sold them for huge profits when prices soared. But he did not consider himself in the real estate business. "It was nothing more than a personal investment," he says.

Building a Long-Term Sustainable Enterprise

In 2000, Michael bought the Fortune Automobile Racing Club from a professional car racer. Due to poor management, the club was on the verge of bankruptcy at the time. Contrary to his previous business operations, Michael decided to build up a long-term sustainable enterprise. He made this investment for two reasons: it was cheap; and the prospects for automobile and sports industries both looked good to him. From 2000 to 2002, the auto industry experienced what analysts called staggering growth in China.

In 2002, Michael bought 200 mu (about 13 hectares) of land in the suburbs of Shanghai and began building a racing circuit, which was completed in May 2003. It was Shanghai's first racing circuit and preceded the government-invested Shanghai International Circuit. Michael recruited world-class designers to design the circuit, which complies with international standards and was recognized by the Federation of International Automobiles (FIA) and the International Motorcycling Federation (IMF). Subsequently, Michael set up the Shanghai Heaven Racing Company that rented the circuit to racing teams for practice and leisure driving, and corporations that used the venue for major PR and marketing events. Clients include automobile and tire manufacturers as well as companies implementing team-building programs. Michael was chairman of the company, and a professional management team was hired to oversee the daily operations.

After taking over the Fortune Automobile Club in 2000, Michael began contacting Shanghai Volkswagen and Shanghai General Motors about possible sponsorship deals. By coincidence, Volkswagen Germany, Shanghai Volkswagen Co. Ltd., and the

Shanghai Automobile Group had just established a joint automobile sales company. The general manager of the German side had a good understanding of the effectiveness of using car racing to promote and market brands. They reached a deal and Shanghai Volkswagen became the name-bearing sponsor for the club's Fortune Racing Team. The club subsequently won sponsorships from manufacturers of car oil and parts, such as Castrol, Homark, and Yokohama Tires. Michael later renamed the club the Speedup Racing Club and put it under his personal management.

Developing New Business Models

The initial business model of the Speedup Automobile Racing Club was traditional. The club team received financial support from sponsors and took part in races. Winning races brought media interest and coverage, thereby boosting the brand name of sponsors and attracting more sponsors to the club. This model was initially quite successful, and the Volkswagen Fortune Racing Team was one of the most established teams in China due to its early start. The team won numerous titles and had many sponsors, but a growing number of racing teams emerged backed by companies such as Nissan, Toyota, Citroën, and Hyundai. Competition grew not only for sponsorship and investment dollars, but also for core competencies of the racing team. Michael explains:

> *The involvement of other auto manufacturers rapidly improved the level of racing teams. It wasn't just a matter of money, it was also about technology. Technology plays a crucial role in car racing. The local technology in this area is rather backward. All these racing teams received technological support from foreign automakers.*

To meet the challenge of the new competition, Michael began trying out new strategies and means of generating revenue. One source of inspiration came from Formula One promoter Bernie Ecclestone. In 2000, Bernie signed a 100-year contract with the FIA to manage and promote Formula One races. Michael notes, "F1 races are enormously popular these days, but it's not the FIA that plays an essential role in this success, instead it's Bernie, the promoter and packager."

The enormous popularity of the Formula One races translates into huge profit for promoters. Those countries wanting to host FIA Formula One World Championship races must apply through Bernie's Formula One Administration (FOA). The FIA collects an administrative fee of US$100,000 for certifying the safety of the track. Hundreds of millions of dollars generated annually from the F1 races fill the coffers of Bernie's FOA. Seeking to duplicate this success, the Speedup Automobile Racing Club's racing department, which coordinated the team's participation in national car races, began to play the role of a race promoter. On behalf of the club, the department reached a deal with China's Federation of Automobile Sports of China (FASC) to promote its two major races.

Starting in 2006, Michael turned the club's six departments into six independent profit centers. In addition to its racing department, Speedup Automobile Club also had departments for sponsor recruitment, PR, marketing and logistics, automobile modification, and race driver training. The marketing and logistics service department played the role of an agent for international brands' car race products. It is also responsible for the development and sale of the Volkswagen Fortune Racing Team's racing jackets, souvenirs, and other items. Thanks to winning numerous national championship titles, the club has gained a certain brand value. The automobile modification department was established to make use of this factor. The race drivers department is commissioned by the FASC to offer training for professional racecar drivers. In 2005, about 70% to 80% of newly certified professional race drivers in China were trained by the Speedup Automobile Racing Club.

Integration of Value Chain Resources Six years is not a long time in the development of an ordinary enterprise, but it was long enough for the Speedup Automobile Racing Club to earn large sums in the value chain, which included sponsors, car racers, fans, media, and the FASC. Speedup's name-bearing sponsors include Volkswagen, Yokohama Rubber, Red Bull, Homak, and Cusoco. Its top driver, Wang Rui, was ranked number one by the FASC for three consecutive years. Response to the training program has been so good that Michael plans to open the first auto racing school in China. In addition to professional racecar drivers, the school will also train much-needed technicians for modification, maintenance, and repair. Michael has already begun talks with a school in Songjiang about possible cooperation.

Since car racing is so popular with the public, it often receives much media exposure. Due to its excellent performance in national-level races, the Volkswagen Fortune Team has a large fan club, which has won more fans and more media coverage. Speedup also has its own magazine, *Speed*, which is distributed to members. The fan club and magazine contribute to the club's brand identification.

Looking into the future five to ten years, Michael displays the flexibility of a typical Wenzhou businessman. In his view, new investment and players will continue flowing into China's automobile racing market, creating increasingly intense competition. Michael says:

I'm very open-minded about this. The bottom line is to achieve win–win results with a strong partner. I don't care who the partner is or how the alliance is formed. The most important thing to me is to keep strengthening my enterprise. If I can keep the leading position in the industry, I'm sure there will be offers of cooperation.

Challenges

Michael admits that the biggest challenge for the Speedup Automobile Racing Club was the difficulty in finding skilled management talent. His entire management team has been internally trained and promoted from within the organization. The decision to turn the six departments into profit centers meant that department heads needed to run the business independently. Were they up to the task? Did the departments possess the necessary organizational capabilities for a profit center?

The Story of Liu Qiongying

Starting from Scratch

Liu Qiongying was born into a farming family near Chengdu, Sichuan Province. Her father worked in a factory in town while her mother took care of the family farm. At a young age, Liu felt her parents' hardships and heavy burden, so she began to do chores such as fetch well water by the time she was eight. In 1986, after finishing junior high school, Liu invested RMB 600 to rent a small three-meter room to sell shoes, marking the start of her business career.

Liu furnished the bare room that was tucked behind a barber's shop with modest shelves to display the shoes. Riding her bike to two suppliers in Chengdu, Liu was able to bring back only a few pairs of shoes at a time. Although the store was shabby, Liu began to do a brisk business, charging two or three times the RMB 30 or RMB 50 cost of the shoes.

At that time, tastes in fashion were still basic but demand for more expensive and fashionable goods was emerging. The following year, business was good enough for Liu to take over the barber's space and her store size doubled, allowing her to expand her product line from gym shoes to leather shoes for men and women. At that time, leather shoes were considered a real luxury as most people still wore canvas or synthetic shoes.

By the third year, Liu had learned to bypass wholesalers and went directly to small shoe manufacturers. Since leather shoes were still fairly scarce, Liu only had access to a small supply. To solve the problem, Liu bought candy that was considered a luxury and gave them to a few key people who handled orders. Afterward, whenever new styles of shoes were introduced, these key people made sure to reserve a dozen pairs for Liu.

In the same year, Liu purchased another store with a total of 75 square meters and named it "Daqiao Footwear Store." A year later, realizing that supply problems were putting her business at a disadvantage, Liu decided to approach the shoemakers with a proposal. While entertaining the owners, she asked if she could promote their brands by exclusively selling their products. An agreement was made and she had access to first selection on new styles and products.

As her retail operation grew, Liu began considering getting into the wholesale business. In addition to the two stores she had already acquired at Zuoqiao, Liu also ran a 90-square-meter store with nine employees. So, she rented a store at Jiaotong Road and began to operate a retail and wholesale business at the same time. The sourcing of suppliers was no longer limited to those around Chengdu but spread as far away as Guangzhou, Shishi, and Jinjiang. In 1991—a year before economic reform began following Deng Xiaoping's visit to southern China—21-year-old Liu made her first million yuan. For most people who earned an annual income of under RMB 1,000, reaching the million RMB mark was beyond imagination. Thirty years of planned economy had dampened the spirits of the few that dared to dream but no longer had the courage to take the first step.

While operating her wholesale business, Liu witnessed first-hand the astounding growth of small-time shoe suppliers when it dawned on her to start her own large-scale manufacturing plant. In 1995, Liu purchased a three-mu (about 2,000 square meters) plot and started the construction of her own shoe factory that went into operation a year later. Benefiting from established relationships she had with retailers and distributors over the years, her first year as a shoe manufacturer went fairly smoothly. Retailers and distributors from Shenyang, Harbin, Xian, Lanzhou, Wuhan, and Hangzhou all came with orders in hand, which brought in sales of RMB 3 million the first year.

In the second year of operation, the company was overwhelmed by problems of quality control and uncollected payments. Cracked soles accounted for RMB 3 million worth of returned goods, pushing the company close to bankruptcy. At the end of the year, Liu personally visited three big clients and returned with only part of what the company was owed. Once her employees were paid, there was little left to pay her suppliers. Problems with quality struck again in the summer of 1998, causing orders to suddenly evaporate.

Around this time, the financial crisis in Russia began to abate and reports spread about how easy it was to do business in Russia. Faced with stiff competition at home, Liu packed a suitcase and some shoe samples and traveled to Moscow. There she found an interpreter, and the two of them spent three months visiting markets during the day and sleeping in dorms at night. Liu returned to China with several orders.

Although the first overseas order was small, the profits Liu made revived her dying shoemaking business and set Aiminger Leather Goods Manufacturing Company on track to becoming a shoe exporter. Once the channel to Russia was opened up, Aiminger continued its push into Eastern European countries such as Lithuania, the Czech Republic, and Ukraine, as well as in Central Asian countries, such as Kazakhstan, Kyrgyzstan, and Turkmenistan. Of the products sold there, approximately 50% carried Aiminger's own brand, and the remainder were sold under private brands.

In 2000, in preparation for its eventual accession to the WTO, China began easing its controls over international trade. Entities wishing to import and export only needed to be registered and not licensed, a change that was a boon for private investors. Under the previous system, it was almost impossible for private businesses to get licensed for foreign trade. Later that year, Aiminger became the first private-owned manufacturing business to be granted the right to engage in import and export operations.

Excited about the prospects for new business, Liu began exploring the international market, with the United States as her first target. She researched woman's footwear companies at a New York library and found a Chinese interpreter who happened to have trading experience in China. Armed with a list of potential clients, the two contacted the top five companies and followed up with visits. One company, a small distributor, became a client right away and eventually became a good and steady client. A second company, a larger trader, showed interest and sent a team to make an appraisal of Aiminger and its product quality. Although Aiminger passed the quality test, its management was not up to par. Liu kept in touch with this second company even though no business was generated. In 2006, the company's vice president and four senior executives made an inspection visit to Aiminger's facilities and Liu remained convinced that she would receive an order from this company in 2007.

Liu also attended trade shows in the United States to win business. One time a trade show participant approached Liu and criticized her for being at the trade show, accusing her of being there to steal designs. But once he saw Liu's samples, he was appreciative of the styles and quality of Aiminger's products and his company later became a client.

Performance + Efficiency + Emotional Input

Whenever a new manager or sales member joins Aiminger, he or she will likely spend a month learning about the production process by making two pairs of shoes by hand. Each employee, therefore, knows that there were over 106 procedures to make a pair of shoes. It not only gives employees a working knowledge of production, but also prepares them psychologically for the job. Managers are able to identify problems and know how to solve them. The practice also earns managers respect from those on the production line, allowing for better communication between the two. In fact, the most important criterion for the promotion of workers to the managerial level is the person's ability to appreciate and relate to the team.

Liu's philosophy on psychological and physical training for management are expressed as follows:

The main benefit is the cultivation of teamwork, the tipping of a person's psychological balance mostly comes from comparison. Take for example the feeling that arises when someone else appears to be making or getting more than oneself, or the feeling one gets when one contributes more than others. The cultivation of the mind and body is designed to change this "comparison-prone" mentality so that one maintains the state of mind that within a team, one's contributions vary with projects, periods of time, and phases of procedures.

Aiminger has had a relatively stable management team. Apart from management training programs, the company also ran management programs to exercise both the body and mind. The first type included cost control, performance evaluation skills, and leadership capabilities; the second type involved exercises designed to improve the psychological and mental wellbeing of the management team, usually provided by psychologists as well as the Deputy Chair of the Hong Kong Association of Believers in Daoism. In Liu's opinion, people tend to lose their psychological balance when they engage in "comparison thinking." When the contributions are the same for them and others, they tend to feel that others are better compensated, or if the compensations are the same, they tend to regard themselves as having contributed more than others. Since 1999, Aiminger had posted an annual growth rate above 40%. Such fast growth implies that the managerial teams have been given fairly handsome bonuses based on their job performances as managers. In addition, those who continued their employment with the company were given raises ranging from 5% to 10%.

On the issue of promoting an "insider," or a close relation, over a professional manager, Liu believes that consideration should be given to individual ability and not whether one is an insider or not. This was a lesson Liu had learned from years of experience running the retailing business and recruiting sales persons. Management positions at Aiminger's various departments, such as finance, marketing and design, are all filled by managerial professionals with only one exception—the person responsible for procurement. That key position belongs to Liu's husband.

Balance

There is a Chinese saying that states: children from a poor family learn how to run the household from an early age. Liu had come a long way from her poverty-stricken childhood and short-lived education to owning three shoe manufacturing facilities with more than 3,000 employees and revenues of RMB 300 million. As the company moved along in the value chain (from retailer to wholesaler to manufacturing), Liu explains:

> *The most important quality required for a successful enterprise is a sound mentality; that is, to make the people around you happy, to make yourself happy. To achieve this state of mind, the key is to keep a balanced schedule and a balanced mind.*

Liu also encouraged the members on the management team to honor their parents and treat them with respect and gratitude. She feels that expressing gratitude is more than simply giving away gifts or money, but instead what gives parents more joy is visiting them and having the family together.

One cannot avoid bad things from happening such as mistakes and wrong strategies that lead to losses. Commonly, bosses tended to internalize the pressures felt during bad times. Liu chooses to maintain her perspective by recalling the Spring Festival celebrations during her childhood. Even though those days were the poorest of her life, she felt joyful when visiting neighbors with her pockets full of candies and roasted sunflower seeds. She recalls those times as being some of the brightest in her life. Despite now having great wealth, the most important thing to her is, "health and happiness, not how much you've gained or lost."

New Challenges

Upon breaking into the Western European market in 2000, Aiminger discovered that the needs of the clients there differed from those in Russia. To meet the demands of the new market, Aiminger had to come up with different designs and styles. To address the problem, Liu established an R&D center in Guangzhou—the shoe industry hub in China. Because the R&D center's requirements for raw materials was low, suppliers were reluctant to do business with it. Instead of giving up, Liu established a manufacturing plant and warehouse and moved the R&D center into the facilities, integrating the development, production, and logistics under one roof.

Aiminger grew into a manufacturing business with a relatively strong R&D team with 40 well-known designers, more than 3,000 newly developed products, and over 90 mould-making professionals. In the meantime, the company also utilized overseas design talents to develop products for its own labels—both an Italian Design Center and a Spanish one were contracted to work on the designs for some of Aiminger's products.

Among its exported products, 70% were under private labels, the remaining 30% were traded under Aiminger's own brand. The company's profit margins were above average and the dominance of shoes under private labels was the main reason. Aware of this, Liu deliberately increased Aiminger's R&D expenditures to create the company's own brands.

As China's economy began rapidly developing, the level of domestic consumption began to rise. Since 2005, Liu has been closely watching the domestic market with the hopes that Aiminger will one day sell shoes to the Chinese under its own brand name. As of the end of 2006, Liu was faced with uncertainties. Could she begin business in domestic retailing? As a brand, did Aiminger wield enough power and influence? What market position should Aiminger aim for? With its business in foreign trade, did Aiminger have what it takes to support a retail operation?

The Story of Hou Zhengyu

Entrepreneurship Experience

Hou Zhengyu was born into a farming family in Hongze County in Jiangsu Province in 1969. As his grandparents and parents were members of the Nationalist Party, they were frequent targets of denunciation at mass gatherings on "class struggle" during the Cultural Revolution. Yet his family provided some important life lessons; they instilled in him at an early age the importance of setting big goals and dealing with setbacks and difficulties in one's life with a positive attitude.

Hou studied management science in a vocational school and stayed on as a student teacher for a year upon graduating in 1989. He then took up the post as an assistant manager at the school-operated factory—another ambitious young man inspired by the "commercialization wave" that swept the nation. It was during this period that Hou suffered his first setback. His girlfriend broke up with him because his income, at RMB 100 a month, was too low to offer her security. After wavering for a few months, he decided to quit his managerial job and head to Shanghai to become a contract worker in the Hudong Shipyard.

He was determined to change his fortunes and dreamed of the day that he could return to his hometown a successful and wealthy man and reclaim the love of his girlfriend. Hou arrived in Shanghai in 1992, the same year Deng Xiaoping made his South China speeches. The opening-up policy for the Pudong New District had already been underway for two years, and Hou could keenly sense that this was a hotbed for reform and that Shanghai held many opportunities. He returned to school for two years and earned a diploma, studying business management while working as a safety inspector at the Hudong Shipyard. At the shipyard, he noticed that many of the workers were migrant workers and former farmers, and that there was an increasing number of foreign enterprises coming to Shanghai. It struck Hou that these foreign enterprises also needed assistance to recruit workers.

In 1996, the Hongze County labor bureau set up a representative office in Shanghai and hired Hou as a clerk at the recommendation of a relative. In the summer of 1996, after getting word that Far East Containers needed laborers, Hou approached the company with an offer to supply it with workers from Hongze but the offer was rejected. Hou persisted, and after 16 visits to the company and 108 phone calls later the company signed a contract for 62 workers. Although he was able to find the workers from his hometown, he was surprised to learn that in less than a week 50 had quit. Far East Containers demanded compensation over the breach of the contract as it was the first mass departure of laborers in the company's history and caused a huge loss. The laborers felt that they were being cheated and demanded compensation to cover their return trip. After a year and a half of negotiations with no resolution, Hou became so frustrated that he contemplated suicide. A friend had paged him with the message: fear no failure and start anew! It gave him strength enough to brace up and start all over again.

Hou reflected on the failed deal and came away with three lessons: his ignorance of labor laws and regulations as well as his lack of understanding of the contract and the consequences of signing the contract; the problem of logistics—the lodgings for the workers were so inadequate that the farmers found them uninhabitable; and the inadequate vocational skills of the farmers-turned-workers. The third point was the most important factor. In general, these laborers were not well educated and had a low level of vocational skills; they therefore had little chance of passing the three-month probation period.

Hou's contract with Far East Containers was similar to that of most labor agencies at the time. Agencies were responsible for the recruitment and provision of laborers, and were not required to seek a certain level of skills or offer training prior to employment. Furthermore, most of the labor agencies did not provide support such as room and board, and although Hou's agency provided lodgings, their conditions were abysmal. As a result of all these factors, the dispatched workers could not meet the requirements of the employer.

Aware of his failings, Hou began to study labor law and related regulations as well as trying to figure out a better service model. There were two major considerations in the new model: the dispatched workers would be equipped with professional skills required by the employers; and comprehensive logistics services would be provided to the dispatched migrant workers.

In 1997, Japanese manufacturer Ricoh needed to recruit 80 production line operators and quality control inspectors for its fax-machine plant in the newly developed Jinqiao Export Processing Zone in Pudong. Hou tested his new business model and successfully recruited a group of technical school graduates from Hongze who already possessed a certain level of skills, supplemented this with additional training specific to Ricoh's requirements, and provided the logistics for the workers. The case was a success and established Hou's reputation among foreign enterprises in the Jinqiao area.

In 1998, the Jiangsu provincial labor bureau set up an administrative agency in Shanghai to centralize the administration of various county offices. Hou, who by then had moved up the ranks to vice director in the Shanghai office of the Hongze county, was selected to head the new agency. In 2000, under a privatization campaign, Hou's administrative agency underwent restructuring and was renamed Tongda, with Hou as the executive vice general manager. Given Hou's new business model, Tongda quickly became the leading labor service provider for enterprises in the Jinqiao Export Processing Zone, Waigaoqiao Free Trade Zone, and Zhangjiang High-Tech Park.

In 2002, China's employment and HR specialist services market was opened to the private sector. Hou resigned from Tongda a year later and registered his own company—Bridge HR, which quickly grew to five branches by 2007. Bridge HR's annual growth rate reached 130% in revenue and maintained a 27% to 30% profit margin.

Vertical Integration

China's labor placement market[1] was opened to private enterprises in 2002 and to foreign investment in 2003.[2] The influx of these two new groups made competition increasingly intense. SOE giants, such as Foreign Enterprise Human Resources Service Company (FESCO) and China International Intellectech Corporation (CIIC), focused on the high-end lucrative markets of white-collar professionals and high-level executives. Joint ventures with foreign investment mostly targeted the high-end headhunting market. There were almost no big players in the low-end blue- and grey-collar segment. Players in this market, although big in number, were mostly competing on a low-price strategy; the quality of service was generally poor and there were no established brand names. Bridge HR stepped into this market and, unlike its competitors, it concentrated on a niche segment: foreign manufacturing enterprises based in Shanghai and its surrounding areas in the Yangtze River Delta region, especially electronics and equipment manufacturers. Furthermore, the workers dispatched through Bridge HR are mostly graduates of vocational and technical schools who had special technical training.

Bridge HR's supply chain consists of upstream labor resource suppliers and downstream foreign enterprise customers. At the supply end, since foreign enterprises need workers with special skills, vocational school graduates are an ideal resource. Bridge HR secured long-term deals with over 50 vocational schools in Jiangsu. Hou also co-invested with the local government in two national key vocational schools. Hou's hometown, Huaian, is a city with a big agro-industry. Since the mid-1990s, the local government had released a series of policies to promote labor export. These include subsidies for the training of rural laborers and rewards for rural labor export. An RMB 100 subsidy is provided for the training of each worker and an RMB 10 reward is offered for the export of one worker. Bridge HR's labor dispatch and vocational training operations enjoy policy support as well as government subsidies. Since it supplies well-qualified workers to foreign enterprises, Bridge HR is often able to successfully compete against its lower priced competitors. Moreover, it has become a long-term partner of big international companies such as Samsung and Ricoh.

At the customer end, Bridge HR hosts regular HR club events at which well-known professors, experts, and HR directors from major companies are invited to speak. HR staff from many of the foreign companies are also invited. It has proven an effective way to establish Bridge HR's brand name as well as to gain access to potential customers. By 2007, Bridge HR's market share in the labor dispatch service for foreign manufacturing companies in the Pudong New District of Shanghai had exceeded 25% (18,000 dispatched workers). The total number of its dispatched workers in the Yangtze Delta region reached 100,000.

China's fast economic growth saw continued expansion of foreign investment in China. This contributed to the steadily growing labor demands of foreign enterprises. Because of this high demand, foreign enterprises operating in China have become dependent on labor dispatch agencies, showing loyalty to those agencies that provide satisfactory workers and services. These two factors have enabled Hou to practice a "demand–pull" supply chain management, under which the training and recruiting of workers are based on the requirements of the recipient enterprises. For example, at the beginning of 2002, Philips informed Hou that it would need 100 machine operators in August. The workers had to have some basic knowledge of electronics and computer science as well as adequate technical English. Hou immediately passed the message on to his vocational school partners, who recruited and trained workers in accordance with Philips' requirements. After being dispatched to Philips, they quickly became accustomed to their jobs and all of them passed the qualification tests after the trial period.

HR Management of Bridge HR

As an HR service provider, Bridge HR is professional and creative in its internal HR management, for which it placed much emphasis on professional expertise. Since its services targeted foreign enterprises based in Shanghai, Bridge HR required the following professional skills from its employees: proficiency in spoken English, familiarity with the operations of foreign enterprises, and full knowledge of the HR profession and related government policies. "All new recruits must have an educational background in HR management or business administration," says Hou. "Mid- and top-level managers must have work experience in HR management."

In addition, Bridge HR gives high priority to employees' recognition of its corporate culture. Bridge HR's mission statement is: customers are satisfied with the service; shareholders are satisfied with their investment returns; employees are satisfied with their career development. Bridge HR even tests interviewees' comprehension of its mission statement during job interviews. Hou states:

If the interviewee can't put the customer first or the shareholder second, we won't hire him or her. Many of them tended to put human resources first. We would give them five minutes to reconsider. If they again couldn't provide the right answer, we would give them another five minutes. We hire only those who totally share our mission statement.

Hou believes the seemingly simple method was a way of testing employees' recognition of Bridge HR's values. "Those who can recognize our values often excel. Those who can't probably leave after the probation period," he adds.

Many of Bridge HR's top managers have had work experience with big international companies. Of the 198 members of the management team, 21 were from international companies. Some had even reached the level of HR director before joining Bridge HR. A vice general manager was previously the HR director of Suzhou Samsung Electronics, one of Bridge HR's key customers. Why would they give up a stable job and high pay in an international company to join a startup like Bridge HR? Hou believes there are factors other than money, career development, and personal attachment to consider in attracting and retaining talent.

Hou explains that for native Chinese managers working in foreign-owned enterprises, there is a so-called glass ceiling, but not at Bridge HR, which has a more expansive development potential. Hou also has a way of nurturing personal attachments with his new senior managers. "If I can learn from him, I'll treat him as a teacher. If he performs his duties well, I'll treat him as a friend. If he can't contribute much to the company, I'll treat him as a guest," Hou says. In addition, Bridge HR also grants shares to top managers, who can expect to be rewarded with even more shares for excellent performance. Mid-level managers can also expect to be granted stock options for their long-term service.

Effective Employment of Government and Policy Resources

In addition to the innovative business model of labor dispatch services and the strategy of vertical integration, Hou's government experience also played an important role in Bridge HR's success. Through his years in government service, he learned how to navigate the different labor agencies and gain a thorough knowledge of relevant policies and regulations.

Hou also had political clout, given his various government posts. He was held up as a national model young entrepreneur by the Central Committee of the Communist Youth League, and State Vice Premier Hui Liangyu had personally signed a written approval for Hou and his business model. These serve as very effective "political cards" whenever he has difficulties in dealings with government bureaucracies.

Hou also keeps close links with related government agencies in Shanghai. One branch of Bridge HR was purchased from the government's labor bureau of Pudong New District, which held a 20% share in that branch.[3] Hou was also an executive director of the semi-governmental Association of Labor Security of Shanghai. The comprehensive logistic service provided to the migrant workers through Hou's labor dispatch model actually helped the Shanghai municipal government's administration of migrant workers. And it gained approval and recognition from government organs in charge of labor and social security and public security issues. The good relationship with related government institutions paved the way for solving various thorny problems concerning the migrant workers. It also gives Hou easy and quick access to the latest changes in related government policies.

Potential Threats

As an experienced industry insider who is familiar with policy issues and the decision-making process of government institutions, Hou remains fully aware that one main threat is the uncertainty of government policies. "There are many uncertain aspects to government policies in China. Constant policy changes are commonplace," he says. "Although we have various solutions to adapt to policy changes, adapting consumes time and effort."

The new Labor Contract Law of China was approved by the National People's Congress in June 2007 and will take effect in 2008. Some of the new provisions in the law can pose a threat to Bridge HR's business model. For example, it stipulates that the labor dispatch agency must sign a contract with dispatched workers for a term of no less than two years. If the labor-leasing company shortens its leasing period, the labor agency will be obliged to pay affected workers' minimum wages in accordance with the local minimum wage standards for the shortened lease period. The labor agency will also be responsible for salaries between the expiration of an employment contract from one company to the beginning of the next if it falls within the two-year period. Another provision requires categorizing workers into the following: temporary, secondary, or substitutes. This was directed at the practice of some foreign enterprises that used dispatched workers in the long term and stable positions to avoid labor contract liabilities and reduce wage costs. These provisions will likely increase the costs of labor placement companies.

Another major threat is from major foreign recruitment companies that are able to access the Chinese market through joint ventures with local companies. In 2006 alone, three overseas recruitment companies from the US, Japan, and Holland—the biggest in their respective countries—entered China in this manner. The US giant, Monster, partnered with ChinaHR.com, Recruit joined forces with 51Job, and Randstad with Talent Shanghai. For the time being, they are all positioned in the high-end headhunter market. The two domestic giants for talent recruitment and labor dispatch services—FESCO and CIIC—both focus on recruitment and dispatch services of white-collar workers and the high-end headhunter service and are not direct competitors of Bridge HR. However, Hou is considering expanding into their territory:

We won't limit ourselves in the blue- and grey-collar labor services. We'll move up the value-added market of white-collar recruitment and dispatch services. As we have better cost control, we expect our profits will be better than theirs.

In terms of capital power, Bridge HR cannot compare with either FESCO and CIIC or international companies. Their earlier presence in the high-end market is an advantage that is hard to overcome. Furthermore, the core competence of Bridge HR is in blue- and grey-collar workers; expanding into new territory would require restructuring of its core competencies, which is difficult to accomplish within a short period of time.

Notes

1. "Labor market" includes employment agencies for blue- and grey-collar workers, HR specialists for professionals and managers, and the headhunters for top executives.
2. Foreign investment can only enter China's labor market in the form of joint ventures. And foreign shares of the joint venture cannot exceed 49%.
3. Currently, the labor bureau is still a shareholder of Hou's branch company.

PART III

UNDERSTANDING ENTREPRENEURS IN TODAY'S CHINA

CHAPTER

Who Are the Typical Entrepreneurs?

W hat kind of person is a typical entrepreneur? What characteristics does he or she have? There are many discussions on this
topic. During the Wharton Entrepreneurship Conference 2006,
Sam Hamadeh, founder and CEO of the New York–based career
information company Vault.com, brought up the idea that outsiders, such as those of minority groups, immigrants, and homosexu-
als, were more likely to start up a business. President and CEO
of California-based Guardian Mobile Monitoring Systems, John
Tedesco, supported the view by citing opposite cases. He pointed
out that very few established and financially secure people quit
jobs and start their own businesses. This view is based on the idea
of opportunity cost: those who possess much face high opportunity
cost; those who possess nothing lose nothing if they fail, but they
would change fundamentally were they to succeed.

It is easy to imagine that socially and financially insecure people are more likely to start a business of their own. But among the
20 entrepreneurs we interviewed for this book, only some of them
fall into this category. To offer a clear picture as to the differences
between China and Western countries on the topic of "Who is more
likely to start up a business," we classified the backgrounds of the 20
Chinese entrepreneurs into four types:

• Grassroots: lacking financial security and social status.

- Experts: accumulating plenty of expertise/experience in a particular industry.
- Government officials: quitting a political career to start a business.
- Professional managers: accumulating experience in MNCs and having achieved the executive status.

Entrepreneurs of Grassroots Background

As we have mentioned in Part I, one of the criteria we set for our sampled entrepreneurs is that they should not be from a financially or politically privileged family background. In this sense, all of the interviewed entrepreneurs are from ordinary families that can be divided into: those from poor families who were determined to improve their lives from an early age; those unable to secure a satisfactory job or were unemployed after graduating from college and resorted to starting their own business; and those with a rebellious spirit who sought to break from traditional SOEs and start their own business.

Cao Xianglai, General Manager of Hainan Zhongxin Chemical, is typical of the first category of entrepreneurs. He was one of four children born to a poor family in rural Hubei Province. As a boy, he had the privilege of getting an education, and proved himself a conscientious student despite the difficult conditions. Because of the isolated location of his home, Cao walked two kilometers to and from elementary school every day, alone. When he reached junior high school, which was 15 kilometers from his home, Cao boarded at the school and returned home for only one night each week, making the four-hour journey there and back by foot. During these long walks, he contemplated his family's poor circumstances and made a vow to change his destiny and lift his family from poverty.

In 1984, Cao passed the college entrance exam and was admitted into the Wuhan Engineering College, which admitted only 5% of applicants a year. He was the first person from his village to enroll in a post-secondary school. After graduating with a degree in machinery, he was assigned to a state-owned machinery factory. Until the mid-1990s, all college graduates were assigned by the government to SOEs or government institutions. SOE employees received equal shares regardless of the amount of work that was accomplished (in the so-called "communal pot" mechanism) and they had to deal with very complicated interpersonal relationships.

At the end of 1988 after less than six months at the job, Cao quit and went to Hainan to seek better opportunities. Although he knew little about Hainan at the time, this came at the heels of the establishment of Hainan as a new special economic zone (SEZ). Cao was not alone. Hainan became a hot spot for Chinese intellectuals and young college graduates, and it was said that "100,000 people rushed to Hainan." In fact, the actual number likely surpassed 100,000 given that the Hainan Talent Exchange Center, the province's recruitment agency, had 180,000 registered personnel in its records and not all new arrivals bothered to register.

Cao's first few years in Hainan were difficult. He did what he could to earn a living, including selling streetside snacks such as sugar-cane and working on demolition teams in construction. Another early job was working at a foreign trading company, which was an important step that put him on his eventual path: building a trading company for chemical products.

Cao's memories of poverty left an indelible imprint that continues to linger. Like others who share his background, Cao refrains from borrowing money for business and he internalizes any pressure. "My parents borrowed money to pay for my schooling. The creditor came to our home during the Spring Festival asking them to repay the loan. The painful experience of facing a debt collector is engraved in my memory. It's become a matter of principle for me to avoid borrowing money as long as I have other choices," Cao says. "Yet on the other hand, I like lending money. It not only helps someone out, but it proves that I have the means to do this." But this attitude has hampered his ability to enjoy his business success as he continues to feel a lack of financial security.

Lu Wenlong, President of Hightex in Hangzhou, also came from a poor rural family. He shares with Cao a deep-seated desire to make a difference in his life but not Cao's self-imposed pressure. Lu's enthusiasm for business arose from a natural disposition and not a sense of responsibility that motivated Cao. Lu was also a good student in junior high school, but the quota in his village for places at senior high school was only two, which were given to children of cadres, so he continued to study on his own. His favorite topics were science and engineering, and he enjoyed tinkering with ideas and fixing and repairing things by hand. While helping the family with the farmwork, Lu continued to look out for money-making opportunities.

He transported ducks 20 to 30 kilometers by bike to the market in Hangzhou when he was 15 years old; he also painted rusty old bikes to make them look new again. A few years later, he recruited some friends to help him gather and transport some stones to sell to a factory that was under construction. His endeavors reflected a good business sense and confidence.

At the age of 18, Lu became a teacher at a rural high school, teaching physics and math. Five years later in 1983, he quit and got a job in a local TVE—a textile mill. "The only hope to become a millionaire and billionaire is through running a company. You'll never get rich by teaching," he told himself at the time. Lu joined the factory with a goal in mind: to become its director within a couple of years, and he was quite certain he could achieve it. Two years later, he got the contract for the management of the mill and essentially became the director. Back then, due to inefficient management, the factory was heavily in debt and Lu's proposal was quickly approved by the owner (the township government). Within three months, his management proved successful and he signed a contract with another TVE. By the end of 1989, Lu left the TVEs and founded his own company. "No matter how well you do in running contracted TVEs, most of the money you earn goes into someone else's pocket," Lu says. The network, customer resources, and management skills that he developed in the six years laid a solid foundation for his entrepreneurship.

The General Manager of Tianjin Longtaixiang Metal Products Company, Song Qiang, was also from a poor family. What's more, instead of spending his childhood under the care of his own parents, Song was brought up by relatives. At a very young age, he learned to be sensitive to other people's reactions and to be careful about behaving himself. "I always avoided being disliked by other people. I tended to be very considerate of others when dealing with people," Song notes. This characteristic, however, has become a valuable asset in his business dealings.

Longtaixiang is in the business of importing and processing scrap metal for sale in the local market as raw material. Since waste imports are under strict state control, this kind of business requires approvals from various government agencies and frequent contact with customs officials. Although this might be a deterrent for most people, Song was a natural in dealing with government officials, forming good relationships along the way. In his view, government officials were no different from businessmen. Customs officers were familiar with government policies and helped trading companies with their imports and exports. They were essentially acting as consultants but not receiving any fees. "I never forgot their help whenever I made money in the import business," Song says.

Chang Xuehong, General Manager of Shanghai Compass Global Freight, started his own business because he could not find a satisfactory job. He graduated from the Dalian Maritime University in 1990 with a major in navigation but was unable to realize his dream of traveling the world by sea. Instead, he got a job on a domestic ship with the Shanghai Marine Bureau, where he stayed for only one year. He then took on a teaching post at the Shanghai Transportation School, but his monthly salary was only RMB 100, enough to live on but not enough so he could save any money to visit his parents. After two years, Chang knew he had to make a change. At that time, the central government announced plans to open up and develop Pudong New District in Shanghai, and in preparation for his next move Chang took a course on foreign trade.

At the beginning of 1993, Chang joined a subsidiary of the China Ocean Shipping Company (COSCO), which engaged in foreign trade including the trade of vessels. In an SOE such as COSCO, however, there was a strict quota of the number of regular staff. As it could not enroll Chang as a regular employee, his career development would be hindered. As a result, he left COSCO and got married, although he was jobless.

In 1994, together with several friends, Chang turned to some sporadic shipping business. But they couldn't secure any permanent customers. In the second half of 1995, with RMB 100,000 in borrowed funds, they set up a company of their own. Due to their lack of management skills and little knowledge about the market, the business closed after the loss of their only customer. Chang remained jobless for another 10 months, but the experience made him think about how best to run a business. It paved the way for his second business attempt that resulted in his own global freight company.

Lou Xiuhua, Chairwoman of Eitong Air Express, falls under the category of someone with a rebellious spirit wanting to break free of the constraints of traditional systems. A native of Yiwu in Zhejiang Province, Lou graduated from the Zhejiang Sci-Tech University in 1991 and was assigned to the Yiwu General Textiles Factory as a lab assistant. The factory was one of the few SOEs in Yiwu that was highly profitable. The work itself, however, was rather routine and required great patience and vigilance, which Lou found stifling. She was able to complete her work quickly, and then she would go to the nearby small merchandise market, hanging around with friends who were running stalls there. As a punch machine was installed at the gate of the factory, Lou had to climb over the wall to avoid punching out during working hours. When it was about the end of working hours, she would climb back in and punch out at the gate.

The hierarchical system at the factory was typical of Chinese SOEs—complicated, multi-leveled, and based on seniority. There were a number of graduates from Lou's university waiting in line for a promotion, some of them even in their forties. Lou could not envision the next 10 or 20 years in the same position and the same company, and after a year, she quit and headed for Hangzhou.

In Hangzhou, Lou got a job at a POE air-conditioner manufacturer. In the beginning, she performed trivial tasks such as cleaning the office, making tea for other employees, running errands to banks, and such. She was gradually promoted to secretary of the general manager. She left the company in 1994 when she was about to have a baby. Lou learned much from the experience. "It seemed like the opening of a window to me. Every day, there was always something new for me to learn," Lou says. She stayed home to care for her baby for a year, then in 1995 Lou and her husband borrowed RMB 300,000 from relatives and friends and started their own express delivery business.

If poverty can be considered an external factor in a person's drive to start a business, an internal factor might be the belief that "I was born to do something great and I should not waste my time being tied down in one place."

Experts Turned Entrepreneurs

The experts turned entrepreneurs in this book refer to those who accumulated extensive industrial expertise and experience as well as people networks before they started their own businesses. Hou Hailiang is one such person. His Shanghai Original Enterprise Development Co., Ltd. produces rubber and plastic products used in making cables, or polymeric materials in cables. He studied polymeric materials at Hefei University of Technology. Upon graduation in 1984, he was assigned to the Zhengzhou Cable Factory, where he worked his way from an entry level technician to the deputy director of the factory's research center in nine years.

The Zhengzhou Cable Factory was at the time one of the three biggest state-owned cable factories in China and was under the direct supervision of the state's Ministry of Machinery. It had over 10,000 employees, including over 500 in Hou's research center. The job provided Hou with a wealth of opportunities to learn and get hands-on experience. Due to the high status of the factory, being under the state ministry instead of provincial or municipal jurisdiction, Hou was able to attend national-level industry conferences and meet important people in the industry.

One such person was an American-Chinese chemistry professor, who recognized Hou's talent and potential. They became good friends, and the professor tried to lure Hou to leave the SOE and join his company in Tianjin, which Hou did in 1993. At the end of 1994, the company set up a joint venture in Shanghai, and Hou, representing the American side, was vice president of the venture. In 1996, the American side withdrew and sold its shares to the Chinese partner, leaving Hou at a crossroad.

At that time, the development and opening up of Pudong was in its sixth year and there was huge potential in almost every industry. Hou could have gone to the United States with the professor, but instead he chose to start his own business. In 1997, together with two friends he met through business, he began the Original Enterprise Development. Hou chose cable factories as his target market and, given his expertise, he already knew their requirements and what kind of products were not available from existing local suppliers. He then specialized in this product range and placed pricing below that of identical foreign-made items.

Tong Liqun, President of Runway Technology Co., Ltd., is another example of an expert turned entrepreneur. Tong studied communications engineering at university, and upon graduation he was assigned to the Industrial Bureau of the Ministry of Post and Telecommunications (MPT). The bureau administered all MPT's 28 subsidiary enterprises, and was later restructured to form the China Post and Telecommunications Industry Corporation (CPTIC), an enterprise directly under state supervision.

Tong began work as a secretary, and was later moved to the marketing department to work on the campaign "Network Availability at Any Point of Access." It was a huge project, and after two years working on it Tong gained real understanding of the various aspects concerning telecommunication. In 1993, as a pilot project in CPTIC's experiment with self-administered operation, a subordinate company was set up to trade telecom equipment and devices such as telephones, beepers, 1G mobile phones, fax machines, and exchanges. Tong worked nearly two years for this company and became very familiar with telecom terminals. At the end of 1994, he was promoted to vice president of an import company subsidiary to CPTIC, but he and his superior clashed and six months later he resigned and started his own company.

Tong knew that the traditional telecom equipment market—with domestic manufacturers such as Julong, Datang, ZTE, and Huawei, as well as foreign competitors such as Nortel and Alcatel—left little space for him to develop. He positioned his company at the digital telecom industry, which was small. Even today, this segment collects less than 20% of the total revenue made by telecom operators. Back then, its market share was only a few percent. Tong found this industry to be innovation- and technology-oriented, and there was not much competition. These facts made it quite suitable for small companies. A small company has plenty of opportunities once it penetrates into one or two market segments. Based on this vision, Runway Technology started as a dealer in digital telecom equipment. Its main clients are digital bureaus subordinate to telecom administrations from various provinces.

Hou Zhengyu, CEO of Bridge HR, also falls in the category of expert turned entrepreneur because industrial experience is required for his business, more so than agencies specializing in white-collar placements or headhunting services. Hou studied business administration in a vocational school and worked in the school after graduation, first as a student teacher and then as an assistant manager of a factory affiliated to the school. At the end of 1992, Hou left his hometown in Jiangsu Province for Shanghai, and with the help of a relative he got a safety inspector's job in Hudong Shipyard. During this period, he obtained a diploma through self-study. Hudong Shipyard employed many farmers turned migrant workers. At that time, an increasing number of foreign enterprises were burgeoning in Shanghai. It struck Hou that these foreign enterprises also needed solutions to the recruitment of workers.

It happened that in early 1996 the labor bureau of Hou's hometown opened an office in Shanghai. The main function of the office was the exporting of the local surplus rural labor. Hou joined the office and set out to develop a market with a couple of colleagues. In 1998, Jiangsu provincial labor bureau set up an administrative agency in Shanghai to enforce centralized administration on the offices opened by labor bureaus of various counties of Jiangsu. At that time, Hou was already the vice director of the Shanghai office operated by the labor bureau of his hometown county. He was picked by the provincial labor bureau for the position of an office head in its newly created administrative agency in Shanghai. He was later chosen to head the new operations department. In 2000, China's government institutions were required to spin off their commercial operations from their government administrative work. Accordingly, the commercial operations function of the administrative agency Hou worked with was spun off as a separate company: Tongda. Hou acted as the executive vice general manager of Tongda for two years. The six-year experience gained Hou valuable insight into the labor dispatch market and the relevant government laws and regulations. What's more, the first-hand information about the problems of blue- and grey-collar labor services, especially the logistical issues of food and accommodations for off-farm workers, paved the way for the establishment of his labor dispatch services company.

A special figure in our group of experts turned entrepreneurs is Yan Han, President of Hangzhou Wangu Textile Company. Yan's company specializes in the design, development, and weave of yarn-dyed silk jacquard. Yan, however, was not an industry insider; he used to work in the IT industry as a software developer. His knowledge about jacquard's key technology was gained from his software development work.

Yan once worked as a railway switchman and freight handler. He earned a college diploma through attending night school and self-study. Before founding Wangu, Yan and his friends started a small company selling computers and software. In 1992 they began to develop and sell their own CAD software in the textile industry. At that time, all CAD software used in China's textile industry on the design of jacquard was imported at the price of about RMB 1.5 million. Yan's software sold for between RMB 150,000 and RMB 250,000. Yan needed to maintain close contact with clients to customize the software according to their needs, and train their employees to use the technology.

It was from this experience that Yan gained a real understanding of the textile industry, as well as the core technologies of the design and weave of jacquard. "By 1997, we were already the industry leader in jacquard design," says Yan. Despite their success, profits were not satisfactory. "We only got RMB 50 or RMB 60 for each new design, but if I had a textile weaving plant, I could earn several dozen RMB for each meter of fabric. So why not open a textile mill of my own?" At that time, China's silk industry was at a low ebb, and it proved to be a good entry point in terms of timing and opportunity for Yan's shift to the textile industry.

It is evident that one of the characteristics of the expert turned entrepreneur is that all (except for Yan Han) have worked in some SOEs or government institutions for a few years. It was very difficult to start from scratch in the industries they targeted; it requires industry experience and people networks.

Officials Turned Entrepreneurs

Officials turned entrepreneurs is a typical category in China. It does not mean that this group of entrepreneurs have influential family backgrounds in politics. It simply refers to the fact that they have worked for a significant period of time with the government.

Tony Zhang, Chairman and President of Tony's Group, worked at a government post for six years. He studied forestry at the Sichuan Agricultural University, and upon graduation in 1983 he was assigned a job in a county government of Sichuan Province. Chosen as a reserved cadre with good political career prospects, he acted as vice township chief from 1985 to 1987 as part of the training for his future political career. After that, he was moved back to the county government as the director of the administrative office. These experiences greatly improved his social skills and provided him a thorough knowledge of the complicated government bureaucracy.

In 1989, Tony was offered a job with a state-owned trading company in Yibin city. As Tony deliberated whether to accept the job, the county chief tried to talk him out of it. But in the end, government work left him feeling oppressed, and although he could envision himself being promoted and gaining more titles, he did not think the rewards were high enough. He took the new job and did very well. In 1995, he was moved to the Shanghai branch run by the Sichuan Foreign Economic Relation and Trade Commission. A year later, China's foreign trade suffered major setbacks following the government's policy to reduce the tax rebate for foreign traders and then the Asian financial crisis in 1997. Many state-owned foreign trading companies were on the verge of bankruptcy, and the Sichuan Foreign Trade Company faced the same situation. Tony's Shanghai branch, however, contributed 70% to 80% of its total revenue. In the end, Tony paid between four and five million RMB to buy out the company and start his own business.

Michael Ma, General Manager of Shanghai Speedup Automobile Racing Club, is another example of an official turned entrepreneur. Although he was elected Secretary of the Chinese Communist Youth League of his hometown, he had already begun dabbling in private business by starting a home factory. Like other Wenzhou business-men, Michael is not an entrepreneur in the strict sense. His business is not focused in a particular area; instead he engages in anything that guarantees a handsome return, and is often involved in three or five different businesses at the same time.

Officials turned entrepreneurs have a thorough understanding of their situations. They can clearly see their path ahead as a civil servant, but have a less clear idea of their fate if they strike out on their own to build a business; nevertheless, they choose the latter.

Professional Managers Turned Entrepreneurs

The professional managers turned entrepreneurs can be regarded as another unique aspect of Chinese entrepreneurship. Compared with the abovementioned entrepreneurs, those in this category are generally younger. The burgeoning of Foreign Invested Enterprises (FIEs) in China since the mid to late 1990s offered them abundant job opportunities, through which they learned Western business operations and professional managerial skills. When they started their own businesses, they were already well equipped with business expertise.

The General Manager of SPN Technology, Wang Zhi, is from Jilin Province. His family would be considered somewhat "intellec-tual" in China as his father was a pharmacist and his mother was a bank accountant. Wang majored in optical instruments at the Changchun Institute of Optical Instruments, and upon gradua-tion in 1992 he was assigned an R&D job in the Changchun Optical Instruments Factory.

As a Chinese saying goes, "new-born calves are not afraid of tigers." Wang found a newly developed product in the industry and thought that he could design it by himself. He planned with several friends to quit the job and start their own business. After he quit, his friends remained uncertain, thus ending his first attempt at entrepreneurship. The jobless Wang took part in the National Post-Graduate Entrance Exam and was admitted into the Changchun Institute of Optical Machinery, where he earned a master degree in optical instruments.

With degree in hand, Wang in 1998 got a job at a branch of Ricoh in Shanghai in their R&D department. Feeling underappreciated, he left after less than a year. "I came to Shanghai not for a senior white-collar job with any company. Ricoh was just a transition. Ever since my postgraduate days, I made up my mind to start my own business," Wang says. He first tried to look for investment in technologies he earlier developed but no one was interested.

He changed his plans and instead joined a Taiwanese trading company that was an agent for German-made engineering machinery systems. He planned to learn about the market and what it takes to be an agent before embarking on his own path. He worked as a product manager and then was transferred to head the company's Beijing office. He restructured the Beijing team and made development plans for the Beijing market; then he submitted his resignation. "My Taiwanese boss has a very suspicious character. He doesn't trust his staff. I think he transferred me to Beijing to kill two birds with one stone. On the one hand, I was exiled from the core business in Shanghai, and on the other, I could turn the business around in Beijing, which was not doing too well at that time," says Wang.

Wang admitted that he learned a lot from this Taiwanese company, and particularly how a product agent operates. He also came away with a lesson on how to avoid the way his Taiwanese boss managed his company, which resulted from his deep distrust of employees. And at Ricoh, he learned about the Japanese management style. He also observed that the rigid hierarchical structure and over-strict management style can somewhat discourage innovation. After leaving the Taiwanese company, Wang finally realized the dream of setting up a company of his own.

The CEO of Shanghai Xhan Yang Chemical, Cheryl Chen, is from a rather literary family. Her father was a writer and her mother was an editor at a publishing house. After graduating from Shanghai Customs College in 1991, Cheryl was assigned to

Changchun Customs. She did not like the culture of the government institution, and was keeping her eye open for an alternative. She found it in a job working at the Foreign Trade Company of Jilin Province. Owing to her Korean language ability, she was assigned to an office in Korea, where she worked two years importing and exporting wooden products and handicraft items. When the Asian financial crisis was over in 1999, Cheryl returned to China and was employed in a Korean company's Shanghai office. Starting as a grassroots employee, she gradually worked her way up to the position of chief representative of the office.

In 2003, Cheryl's sister, who had already been running her own business for four years, came to Shanghai to expand her business, and persuaded Cheryl to join her. Cheryl agreed, and the two sisters became partners. "My sister is very entrepreneurial. She likes being her own boss. I'm cautious and conscientious and would rather work for others," Cheryl says. In spite of this, Cheryl's Korean language skill, her knowledge and understanding of the Korean culture, together with her experience with Korean companies all made her an ideal partner for her sister. So they established a trading company importing stationery items such as ink and printing ink from Korea.

CHAPTER

8

Business Model

Startup Capital

It was not until 2002 to 2003 that Chinese banks gradually began to offer loans to individual startup entrepreneurs. The banks' criteria for this type of loan was extremely strict. Applicants were required to provide pledges, mortgages, or guarantees, which were usually impossible to obtain. As a result, Chinese entrepreneurs basically could not get a bank loan. Most of our 20 entrepreneurs borrowed from relatives or friends. In addition, there were two other channels to raise the needed money:

- Making the first pot of gold by seizing a golden opportunity.
- Making the first pot of gold by sheltering under a big tree.

Making the First Pot of Gold by Seizing a Golden Opportunity

China's opening up move was accompanied by a gradual transition from a planned economy to a market economy. In this transitional period, market disorder and asymmetric information created many opportunities. Those who recognized the opportunity and had the courage to grasp it often reaped the rewards and made their first pot of gold. Among them was Liu Qiongying, Chairman of Aiminger Leather Goods Manufacturing Company. When Liu started selling shoes in a small shop, she could earn a 300% to 400% profit on shoes purchased at only RMB 30 to RMB 40 apiece. Liu cannot recall the exact figure of her profit for the first year but she is quite certain that it was a very lucrative business.

Business was so good that she was able to double her shop's size in the second year and almost quadruple it the third year. With this pace of expansion, she earned her first million in the 5th year. In the 1980s, the ordinary monthly income of an urban Chinese was just several dozen RMB. Leather shoes and gym shoes were considered luxury goods. At that time, the living standards of the Chinese were rather low, but demand for more expensive and fashionable goods was emerging. This was why the over-100-RMB gym shoes sold so well at Liu's shop. Back then, many Chinese were content with the "iron rice bowl" provided by the SOEs. They did not consider running their own business. The 16-year-old Liu showed great courage in discontinuing her education and starting her own business.

Lou Xiuhua, Chairman of Eitong Air Express Co., Ltd., is another example of someone who made their first pot of gold by seizing a golden opportunity. In the early 1990s, many labor-intensive enterprises in Hong Kong and Taiwan moved to the Pearl River Delta area in southern China by establishing joint ventures. These joint ventures were usually required to make sample goods before mass production. The sample goods needed to be mailed to Hong Kong for inspection and approval. This prompted a huge demand for mailing services between Hong Kong and the Pearl River Delta area. Samples, business documents, and catalogues all require quick delivery, but China Post took three days to deliver a package between the two destinations. This resulted in the fast development of private express delivery services in this region.

Before starting their own business, Lou and her husband both worked at a private air-conditioner manufacturer that also produced air-conditioner parts. Lou's husband was in charge of selling parts to Haier and it often took two days to send sample goods to Haier in Qingdao. As the company was located in a town over 100 kilometers away from Hangzhou, they had to go by boat to Hangzhou to catch a train for Qingdao. The company spent more than RMB 1,000 delivering a sample that was worth only RMB 40 or RMB 50 to make and was sold for only RMB 100. It was then that Lou's husband began thinking of opening an express delivery service.

In 1995, the couple borrowed RMB 300,000 from relatives and set up an express delivery company. Back then, few companies in north-east China were accustomed to using express delivery services despite the fact that the China Post's express service was not very speedy or convenient. After introducing their service, Lou found many companies receptive to the idea. Since there were no competitors or established market prices, they were able to make a handsome profit. In its first year, Eitong Air Express earned between RMB 100,000 and RMB 200,000 in monthly revenues, and their gross profit was 100% to 200%. Lou recalls that the most expensive delivery service at that time was between Hangzhou and Beijing, costing RMB 1,600. Although the China Post's express service was only RMB 21.5, the delivery time was much slower.

Opportunities for Tong Liqun, President of Runway Technology, came from his extensive industrial knowledge and professional know-how. With a communications engineering education, Tong had been in the communications industry for five years when he started his business. He chose to specialize in digital telecom equipment due to the lack of intense competition and big-time players. The traditional telecom equipment market was crowded with all the major players, but the innovation and technology-intensive digital telecom equipment market was more suitable for small companies. Another contributing factor to Tong's selection was the rapid development of the then underdeveloped network infrastructure in China.

As a startup company, Runway Technology did not possess any core technology of its own. Based on his knowledge of the latest technology and products of the industry, Tong chose to act as an agent for companies that had just introduced promising products into China. The first company to hire Runway as its agent in China was Israeli-based Red, whose customers were the digital bureau subsidiaries of the telecom administrations of each province. At that time, the digital telecom equipment market was rather high-end. Market demand was not huge but profit margins were quite high. An RMB 1.2 million order usually netted a 50% profit margin. And monthly sales were always above RMB 10 million.

Runway Technology later made several adjustments to its market positioning to accommodate the rapidly changing technology in the telecom industry. Each of these adjustments was related to new opportunities due to Tong's keen sense in being able to spot and seize upon them.

Song Qiang, General Manager of Tianjin Longtaixiang Metal Products Company, was operating a customs application service company when he came across a Hong Kong plastic wrap importer seeking his assistance. Song came to the realization that the import of waste materials could be a profitable business as it was difficult to place a value on such material. As he was already familiar with the procedures involved in the import of waste material, he was at an advantage. Soon after he began importing waste metal, the global price for raw metal began to rise sharply. Longtaixiang began earning a handsome profit since its second year of operation. And Song, after spotting and seizing the opportunities, thus made his first pot of gold.

Making the First Pot of Gold by "Sheltering under a Big Tree"

As China prepared to enter the WTO, it began liberalizing restrictions in certain industries that were exclusively under the domain of large SOEs that earned huge profits. But due to mismanagement and competition from more efficient operators, many SOEs lost market share or even withdrew from the market. An example can be found in China's import and export industry. Among our interviewees, there were a number who had worked with state-owned foreign trading companies, considered "big trees" in a state-monopolized industry. Under the shelter of these trees, they accumulated experience, built networks, and earned a significant fortune. As the foreign trade industry opened up to competition, many of these budding entrepreneurs left the SOEs and began businesses of their own.

Among those who made their first pot of gold in this way was Cao Xianglai of Hainan Zhongxin Chemical. In 1990, on a friend's recommendation, Cao joined the Hainan branch of the China National Chemical Construction Corporation (CNCCC).[1] CNCCC was one of the two big players in China's chemical import and export industry.[2] The well-known SOE was an excellent platform for Cao, and he worked hard to familiarize himself with every aspect of the operation.

At the end of 1994, due to managerial loopholes typical of an SOE, the Hainan branch of CNCCC suffered a major setback and was shut down. Cao was faced with two choices: he could follow his boss to CNCCC headquarters in Beijing and become a mid-level official, or he could stay in Hainan and run a subsidiary of CNCCC[3] on a contract basis. Cao chose to stay.

As a contractor, Cao had to solve every problem himself, including the lack of capital and personnel. The only support he received from CNCCC was its name. He was, however, able to fall back on the network of contacts he made while working for CNCCC. But in 1996, the government lowered the rate of export tax rebate and this, combined with the Asian financial crisis in 1997, dealt a severe blow for state-owned foreign trading companies. By 1999, Cao could no longer keep the operation afloat and he left the company. He then registered his own business in Hainan. Cao's career at CNCCC—the big tree—allowed him to make a substantial pot of gold. The registered capital for the company, RMB 5 million, came from his own pocket.

As mentioned previously, Tony Zhang of Tony's Group chose a career in foreign trade instead of remaining a civil servant in 1989. By the time he started his enterprise, he had worked with state-owned foreign trade companies for eight years. Compared with Cao Xianglai's CNCCC experience, Tony's time under the "big tree" was shorter, though enough for him to build an extensive network in the industry. His social skills and integrity, which developed during his time in government service, also helped him gain access to key industry people.

In the early 1990s, there was a general lack of information exchange, leaving manufacturers virtually in the dark about the going rates in the domestic and international markets. Tony was often able to obtain the latest market information from his industry insider contacts, allowing him to profit enormously. In one example, Tony purchased five tons of doxycline for RMB 200,000 per ton after finding out about market prices. Within three to five months, the international market price for doxycline soared to RMB 1.5 million per ton, allowing Tony to profit handsomely. Another example involved the development of a new pharmaceutical product. Tony kept up a good relationship with the manufacturer and was among the first to be told of the new product and its benefits. He immediately placed an order and thus gained an early-entry advantage.

In 1997, the parent company that Tony worked for was on the verge of bankruptcy, but Tony's Shanghai branch was doing well, contributing 70% to 80% of the parent company's revenues. It was a natural move for Tony to buy out the company for RMB 4 million. The money came from his saved earnings during his eight years working in two state-owned foreign trade companies—the big trees.

These two channels of raising startup capital—seizing a golden opportunity or taking shelter under a big tree—could succeed only within a particular period of China's transition from a planned economy to a market economy. Some SOEs enjoyed exclusive access to various resources in the planned economy period, acting as an incubator for some of our entrepreneurs. In the meantime, China's reform and opening up policy and its consequent rapid economic development created plenty of golden opportunities for new entrepreneurs to seize and start their businesses.

Business Model

With the exception of the recent "new type of private enterprise" in the IT industry founded by the returning overseas Chinese, concepts such as strategies or business proposals were not really a consideration in the early days of most Chinese private enterprises. The decision to start a company was made when an opportunity was spotted. This pattern is very obvious among most of the 20 entrepreneurs we interviewed. At the early phase of development, they usually adopted a low-cost strategy. When they began to face problems of profit shrinkage caused by increasing competition or when they moved into a new phase of development, they started to adopt strategies such as differentiation, focusing, or integration. Their business model also underwent corresponding adjustments:

- Product/service differentiation
- Focus differentiation
- Niche market
- Vertical integration

Product/service Differentiation

Shanghai Compass Global Freight's main business was as an international freight agency, and it also provided domestic express delivery service. Domestic delivery was used as a supplementary value-added service for Compass's key international accounts. The General Manager of Compass, Chang Xuehong, considered it a competitive differentiated service. This part of the business was essentially treated as an outsourcing service for key clients and Compass employees were stationed within the customers' factories to better meet their demands. The on-site service helped reduce overhead costs and also strengthened customer relationships. What's more, because the cargo was typically of a high value, this sort of express delivery generated a much higher gross profit than others.

Focus Differentiation

Opple Lighting is a manufacturer of household lighting fixtures and lamps. Most players in this industry are small operators, with a few that are medium sized, and most are engaged in the low-end market. Their strategy is to keep production costs low and offer low-cost products. The few big international players focus on the high-end market, such as Panasonic, Philips, and GE Lighting.

When Wang Yaohai founded Opple in 1996, his initial business was the assembly of ordinary lighting fixtures. By the end of 1996, the state government promoted its "Green Lighting Project," introducing energy-saving fixtures to China. Like many of its competitors, Opple entered this area, and by 1998 a fierce price war broke out. It was during this period that Opple established "Quality First" as its strategy. In 1999, Wang registered "Opple" as a brand name and he began targeting mid-market households. Opple products were of a better quality than other domestic brands and lower in price than international brands. Wang successfully established differentiation.

Another aspect Opple worked hard on was the quality of light emitted from its products. Seeing investment into creating innovative designs did not reap huge rewards due to rampant copying, Opple focused its R&D first on producing a high quality of lighting, which was harder to copy, and second on designs, since that is the consumer's first consideration in such purchases. Opple's strategy in focus differentiation proved to be a success. It has become an industry leader with revenues surpassing RMB 1 billion in 2006.

Contrary to Opple, Yan Han's Hangzhou Wangu Textile Company was equipped with advanced technology from the start. From the end of 1994 to 1995, European and American silk markets shrank drastically because of a recession that coincided with a record output of China's silk industry. The sharp decrease in exports led to a huge over-supply of silk in the domestic market, and China's silk industry was dragged into a prolonged recession. On the technological front, most domestic producers used traditional looms. Few of them used computerized design and advanced new looms imported from overseas. Given Yan's textile software development background, he was already on the cutting edge when he launched into the textile industry in 1997 since he possessed the most advanced design techniques for jacquard in China.

China contributes 80% of the world's silk output, but most Chinese silk products are low- to mid-range with little added value. Limitations within this industry are great, and due to intense competition, profit margins are shrinking. When Wangu Textile began exporting silk fabric for ties, it could earn RMB 120 in profit per meter; now that figure is RMB 20.

Wangu's imported advanced looms and latest software designs have placed its products on the high end since it began doing business. Yan believed a company's sustained growth lay in quality rather than quantity. "A natural fabric like silk is a high-end luxury product and shouldn't be targeted at the mass market. The commoditization of the silk will lead the industry down a dead end," he says. In the course of its expansion and growth, Wangu became increasingly focused on the high-end market.

Wangu's Italian business partner is a silk fabric supplier whose clients include some of the top names in fashion. This partnership not only gave Wangu a competitive advantage in weaving technique, but also secured access to the latest trends and technology in color, fabric texture, and patterns. Wangu supplied custom-made fabrics for brands such as Dunhill, Celina, Chanel, and Pierre Cardin. It also produced scarves, curtains, bed textiles, and household decorative textiles bearing its own brand, Mantani. Mantani is also targeted at the high-end market, mainly for export to Europe, and to Japan where its bed textiles can be found alongside names such as Burberry in that country's most exclusive stores. Although Wangu's volume is far lower than other manufacturers, it has a much higher profit margin and its volume remains stable. Its sales revenues in 2005 reached RMB 270 million.

Real estate development is a capital-intensive industry, and this is especially true for large or high-end projects. As a starting-from-scratch entrepreneur, Gao Qi, President of Suzhou Merryland Real Estate Development, was well aware of this so she focused on small residential projects, building her competitiveness based on efficiency. Before a developer can begin work, it must receive certification in four categories, which typically takes six to ten months. Merryland was able to get it done in three to four months, thereby reducing the cash flow cycle on loan repayment and cash requirements for new project development. Merryland's projects are also targeted at ordinary consumers, which are easily sold on the more reasonable prices.

"We complete one-and-a-half to two projects in the time it takes other developers to finish one project," the CFO of Merryland says. Large real estate projects in China are generally over 100,000 square meters, and projects as large as over 200,000 square meters are not rare for big developers. Within four years of entering the real estate industry in 2003, Gao was involved in projects that totaled 400,000 square meters, all of which were small. By focusing on the market of small ordinary residential projects, Merryland achieved rapid development in spite of its limited capital resources.

Niche Market

Hou Zhengyu's success with Bridge HR lies in its positioning within a niche market. China's labor market had been monopolized by government labor and personnel administrative agencies. Since 2000, new policies were gradually introduced, including removing the requirement for residency status and the promulgation of "Regulations on Labor Market." In 2002, China's employment and HR specialist market was completely open to domestic POEs. In 2003, foreign investors were allowed to enter the market in the form of joint ventures with domestic companies.[4] Currently, the highly lucrative HR specialist services market for white-collar workers and headhunting services for senior executives are controlled by the big two SOEs: Foreign Enterprise Human Resources Service Company (FESCO) and China International Intellectech Corporation (CIIC). Joint ventures mostly target the high-end headhunting market. Meanwhile, there are virtually no big players in the low-end labor dispatch market for blue- and grey-collar workers.

It is this market that Hou's Bridge HR chose to target. In addition, Bridge HR further concentrated on the niche market of foreign manufacturing enterprises in Shanghai and its neighboring areas. The workers dispatched to Bridge HR's customers were mostly trained with certain technical skills, with one-third being technical school graduates. Bridge HR satisfied the huge demand for workers with professional skills and gained a competitive advantage over its competitors using low-price strategies. Bridge has also formed a long-term partnership with Samsung and Ricoh. Bridge has dispatched a total of 18,000 workers, and its sales revenues have continued to increase by 130% in the past few years.

Vertical Integration

Hainan Zhongxin Chemical's main business was in the foreign trade of chemical and medical products. When Zhongxin grew to a certain scale, it began to use its technology and brand to integrate the supply chain. At the customer end, with Zhongxin's brand build-up and R&D strength, it upgraded itself from a pure trading agent to an agent combined with certain functions of a supplier: supplying custom-made products to customers. The products were not necessarily made by Zhongxin, even though Zhongxin had its own factories. At the supplier end, when Zhongxin reached 70% to 80% of a supplier's total output, the latter would have a certain reliance on Zhongxin, making it easier for Zhongxin to control prices. In the meantime, Zhongxin's R&D strength enabled it to control suppliers' product quality. After they passed quality inspection, all products were transported to Zhongxin's warehouse for packing.

Zhongxin also began moving into the logistics sector. Logistics cost was usually 20% to 30% of the total trade volume. "My logistics business was not for profit. Firstly, it was to control costs. Secondly, it was to control the quality of the logistics service," says Cao Xianglai. Zhongxin's big international customers all needed to outsource their cargo transportation to professional logistics companies. Zhongxin provided this service to strengthen its link with key customers and lift itself from a single-product supplier to a provider of a package of services. Cao planned to hire logistic professionals to manage his logistic business.

Bridge HR focused on the supply of blue- and grey-collar workers to foreign manufacturers based in Shanghai. Because not all farmers turned migrant workers had the necessary skills, Bridge HR's CEO Hou Zhengyu turned to the operation of technical schools. With support from local governments, Bridge HR formed a partnership with more than 50 technical schools. Bridge also invested in two technical schools of its own. This direct involvement not only enabled Bridge HR to design courses and train workers according to the needs of foreign enterprises, but also guaranteed the supply of technically competent workers. On the customer end of their supply chain, Bridge HR hosts regular forums through its HR club. They invite respected HR professors, experts, and HR directors of large enterprises to give lectures to local HR professionals. In this way, Bridge HR gradually built its brand name among enterprises and secured abundant customer resources. So far, Bridge HR has more than 90% of the market share of blue- and grey-collar labor dispatch services for foreign manufacturing enterprises based in Shanghai.

Business Models with Chinese Characteristics

The abovementioned business models have been generally accepted by businesses around the world. In addition to these, some of the enterprises we feature used business models that are "characteristically Chinese." Because some industries in China are under strict state regulation, relationships play an essential role; this is especially true for POEs.

The Tianjin Longtaixiang Metal Products Company specializes in the import of scrap metal that is then processed and sold as raw metal. As this type of operation is regulated by the government, winning government-approved status requires skilled government relations. Also, as it involves the import of goods, the business involves much interaction with customs officials.

General Manager Song Qiang already had contacts with customs officials due to his previous work with a Sino–Japanese joint venture, and when he began his own business, their relationship further strengthened. Song's social skills and tendency to show consideration for others developed at an early age. This has helped Song build a good network of contacts, which has been invaluable in his business.

Longtaixiang's profits came from two sources; one was in the savings on customs duties and the other was the price difference between scrap and raw metal material. The customs savings could be made because it is difficult to put a value on scrap metal, and since customs duties are calculated on a percentage of the value of goods, it is up to the individual customs official to determine the actual value. When Song entered the market in 2000, he concentrated mainly on the import of scrap copper and aluminum, which happened to coincide with a dramatic jump in global raw metal prices. "The price of copper rose three times and the price of aluminum almost doubled," Song says.

Although Song's profit margin was much bigger than most of the entrepreneurs we interviewed, he has also showed more concern about the company's future than the others. The root of much of his concern was political risk. As China was undergoing a transitional period, the replacement of government officials became more frequent than usual, and this was especially the case among local officials. Worried that the officials within his network might be replaced, Song continued to expand and consolidate relationships. Song notes that officials should not be too highly placed or low–ranking, as those in the lower ranks have little leverage while high-ranking officials may become political targets. "To be honest, I don't like operating this way," Song says. "I wish China had clearly defined regulations. It would be simpler to operate by following the rules. The lack of clearly defined regulations makes our operation relationship-dependent. I don't have a sense of certainty for the future."

Shanghai Zhicheng Communication's main business is telecom engineering projects and its customers are telecom operators. General Manager Cui Lijian admits that relationships are crucial to this line of business and he has his own approach on this issue. Cui has built relationships differently from Song. He often used gifts to build ties, but whereas his competitors would give gifts as valuable as villas, Cui took a more spiritual approach. He notes that most of the influential people in the telecom industry tended to be of an older generation with a relatively low level of education. Cui, meanwhile, had many different interests and hobbies; he had worked in the IT and stock investment fields before founding Zhicheng, and he often conversed with these influential people on a variety of topics such as photography, golf, high-tech, and investment portfolios. In short, he spent time socializing with them and being friends, sometimes offering them advice on camera purchases and inviting them for afternoon tea or coffee.

Cui also hired people to expand his network. One time, an influential person's brother came to Cui looking for work. The brother was immediately hired and given an attractive compensation. In return, Cui found that the brother could get things done more smoothly than other employees. "For example, when we needed to get work done in a client's computer room, our people usually gave small gifts such as packs of cigarettes to those in charge for their cooperation. But if he was there, people would take the initiative to help without any gifts," Cui says. From then onward, Zhicheng gave a high priority in the recruitment of those who understood the local culture and had rich local resources.

Cui also resorted to cunning tactics to further exploit his network. On some occasions, he would casually "reveal the secret" that

Zhicheng was backed by somebody important. "You need to let them feel that you've got an important relationship, but it's got to be a bit of a mystery. Nobody is clear about who's the big figure backing you. This really works. It's saved us from many troubles," Cui says.

In addition to relationships, Zhicheng has its core competencies, which are access to government-approved competency credentials and a high level of efficiency in engineering tasks. Cui applied for credentials soon after starting the company, even though it was not necessary at the time. In 2006, when the state raised the threshold for industry access by requiring competency credentials for telecom engineering businesses, many of the established companies in the industry had not gotten their credentials, creating many opportunities for Zhicheng.

Another issue that Cui worked hard on was expediency on completing a project because they inevitably involved digging up roads, thereby affecting the public. "Efficiency and speed are our biggest advantages," Cui says. Unlike many of its competitors, Zhicheng did not outsource this work and had its own engineering teams and front-line workers. Although it was more expensive than outsourcing, Zhicheng could better control the speed and quality of work accomplished.

It is not hard to see that both Song Qiang and Cui Lijian have worked hard to build and maintain their relationships with key people as dictated by the nature of their respective industries. But neither enjoys operating in this way. They prefer a well-regulated business environment in which they can compete on equal footing based on competency.

American Models Do Not Work

One of the findings of our research is that the business models generally adopted by American entrepreneurs do not work in China. Among them is the venture capital model in the IT industry, which brings us to the story of Chen Xin. Chen received her college education in the United States and worked with IBM and AMD for 10 years as an IC design engineer.

The US business model for starting enterprises is first get a good technology, then find venture capital or angel investment to finance the technology's introduction to the market. If the market response is less than satisfactory, there are always companies interested in your technology so long as it is good technology. In China, this is not the case. Because venture capitalism is relatively underdeveloped, the focus is on the end product or market for the product and not the technology itself.

Chen and her partners began designing network security chips, with their initial financing coming from system manufacturers and angel investors in the US and Taiwan. The Taiwanese investors required that their business be headquartered in Taiwan, and Chen returned to her hometown to head the Shanghai branch. Chip manufacturers in the States are able to collaborate with systems manufacturers to fulfill the requirements on design, but this kind of customized chip manufacturing had not developed in China, as manufacturers simply produced products for an existing market, namely consumer electronics.

Later on, the Taiwanese investors saw a market opportunity for VOIP (voice over internet) equipment and decided to enter this area of business. As the future of VOIP was more tangible, they transferred most of the company's human and other resources to promote, sell, and service this new line of products while chip design was reduced to a smaller role in the business. Since many of the staff members had a background in chip design, the transition was not easy. Chen had been in this tough situation for three years before realizing that, "when in Rome, do as the Romans do." A business in China should always begin with market research, then capital second, and R&D as the last consideration.

Transformation

The typical path of development for POEs in China includes three stages: trader, manufacturer, and technology developer. After spotting market opportunities, our entrepreneurs typically entered the trading sector, such as being an agent for foreign brands. During this stage, they gained market, product, sales, and management experience. The building up of a sales network accompanied the accumulation of capital. This was followed by the mastering of manufacturing techniques and management skills when they entered the second stage of scale production (as OEMs in most cases). In the end, they would invest in R&D to establish their own brand.

The development of China's private enterprises has been determined by both limitations in financial resources and China's

industrial development. Private business startups were charac-
terized by limited funds and human resources so the most viable
form of entrepreneurship was as a trader or agent for name brands.
China's industrialization has been largely aided by the transfer of
manufacturing technology from overseas, and as a result many
trade-oriented private enterprises became involved in OEMs once
they raised enough capital. OEMs provided opportunities for entrepreneurs to master core technologies and build their own R&D.
This laid the foundation for the progression into manufacturing
their own brands using their own technology.

Most of the 20 enterprises we investigated have taken this development path in their growth. According to the different stages, we
divided their transformations into the following categories:

- Transformation from trader/agent to service/solution provider
- Transformation from outsource production to self-production
- Transformation from brand agent to brand owner
- Transformation from sales-oriented strategy to marketing-
oriented strategy
- Transformation from single product line to multi-product line

Transformation from Trader/Agent to Solution/Service Provider

During the early stages of a trader/agent's business, the market
allows for large profit margins and the trader/agent undergoes
rapid growth. As the market becomes saturated and competition
increases, profit margins become narrower and narrower, leading
the trader/agent to shift its role to service or solution provider.

Shanghai KeyPoint Controls started as an agent for instruments
and meters used in the oil and chemical industries. Later, KeyPoint
developed a new business line called professional service that
included the automation of measurement and control in the can-
ning of liquid chemicals. KeyPoint's first line of business was being
an agent for a number of foreign brands, including US-based
Dresser Instruments. Its second line was being a service provider,
cooperating with domestic partners to offer software and services to
customers. Combining the two businesses, KeyPoint could provide
professional package solutions to customers. Although its packaged
solutions are profitable, KeyPoint President Liang Qihua still
plans to build a factory in two years as part of efforts to strengthen

KeyPoint's core competence. Liang plans to assemble products using imported parts according to their customers' needs with their own technical solutions all under their own brand name.

Cao Xianglai's Zhongxin Chemical serves as another example in this category. From 1995 to 2006, Zhongxin's sales revenues soared several dozen times, yet profit was reduced by half, prompting Cao to invest in R&D and manufacturing. The initial investment funded an R&D group at Shanghai Jiaotong University whereby Zhongxin was entitled to any R&D results and achievements. Since 2002, Zhongxin began to establish factories in Guangxi, Tianjin, Qingdao, and Jiangsu. These factories were capable of producing value-added products with self-owned core technologies to meet customers' needs. By the end of 2004, Cao began to transform Zhongxin into a service provider and implemented strategic adjustments in 2005 and 2006. Its business volume and improved R&D competence increased its leverage on the price and quality of suppliers. In the meantime, Zhongxin began to enter the logistics sector to provide custom-made logistics services to its customers. At present, trade still accounts for 90% of Zhongxin's total revenues, though Cao plans to reduce that figure to 60% to 70%, and increase the percentage of its own production to 20% to 30%.

Transformation from Outsource Production to Self-Production

The initial business model of Hou Hailiang's Shanghai Original Enterprise Development was: based on Hou's knowledge of the market and industry, and ability to carry out market-oriented R&D; outsource production of their newly developed material and technology; and sell the products to customers. At the beginning, the sales volume was not huge, but profits were good. After a couple of years, increasing market demand rendered the outsourcing production-based model unable to meet new requirements on output, quality, cost, and production cycle of products. Hou, therefore, decided to build his own factory, and in 1999 he took out a bank loan with the help of some friends and began construction on a factory that was completed in 2001.

Meanwhile, Original Enterprise continued to focus on R&D, and in 2002 the Shanghai municipal government selected one of its products as a high-tech project, giving Original Enterprise the status of a government-subsidized enterprise. Original Enterprise's transformation from outsourcing to production contributed to its rapid growth in 2002 and 2003. However, purchasing new lab equipment and production lines, as well as strengthening R&D, required a huge capital outlay. Like all POEs in China, it was difficult for Original Enterprise to obtain bank loans. In addition, the increased price of oil and other raw materials since 2003 have squeezed their profit margins. To solve its financing problems, Original Enterprise negotiated a joint venture deal with an Italian company in 2004, giving each party a 50% share.

At the time, competition had become increasingly intense. On the technological front, Original Enterprise was an industry leader, but due to the Italian partner's insistence on a high level of quality in raw materials and products, the price of their products was much higher than that of competitors. What their Italian partner did not understand was that many of Original Enterprise's customers did not have high requirements on quality, they preferred more attractive prices. It was a situation characteristic of the Chinese market.

Hou was faced with two choices: expand production by reaching new partnership deals, enabling him to compete on an economy of scale; or integrate the value chain through reaching partnerships with upstream and downstream enterprises.

Transformation from Brand Agent to Brand Owner

"Without its own product, brand or core technology, no company can significantly expand and grow, at least not in our industry," says Wang Zhi, General Manager of SPN Technology. The company's main business is the sale of automatic control systems for engineering machinery. Its products fall into two categories: hardware and software.

In the first two to three years, SPN acted only as an agent of hardware products for European and US companies. During this period, Wang found that the selling of these products required agents who had the ability to provide technical support to integrate its products. This included training customers to use the equipment and the software, as well as helping customers make customized adjustments. SPN began to build an R&D team in 2003 to develop its own software and hardware. To date, most of SPN's software products have been self-developed and the company holds more than a dozen patent technologies. It has also developed some hardware products whose production was outsourced.

At the same time, SPN was gradually building up its own brands. Generally, SPN's domestic customers tended to highly regard European technology and brands. The company registered a company in Germany with the intention of getting the European market familiar with and accepting of SPN's German brand, which would in turn win domestic customers. At present, all of the R&D work and part of the production of SPN's German brand are located in Shanghai and only part of the manufacturing takes place in Germany. Wang plans to transfer the entire production to Shanghai in the future. Different from its domestic competitors, SPN developed a brand for the overseas market as well as the high-end domestic market at a cost similar to a domestic brand. SPN plans to make its own brand its main business while gradually easing its business as an agent for foreign brands.

Of our interviewed entrepreneurs, Liu Qiongying's Aiminger Leather Goods underwent a typical three-stage development of trader, manufacturer, and technology developer. In the course of its development, Aiminger had transformed from an initial domestic retailer and wholesaler to an export-oriented business. Its sales revenue reached RMB 200 million, 70% of which was from OEM production, and 30% was from self-owned brands. Aiminger's R&D team is made up of 40 designers, and the company holds intellectual property rights on over 1,500 technologies. The company also outsources some R&D projects to Italian and Spanish design companies. Because of heavy expenditure in R&D and OEM production, Aiminger's profit margin is in the upper-middle range for the industry. Since 2005, Aiminger began to shift its focus back on the domestic market and it plans to sell its own brand of products locally in the future.

In the case of Hangzhou Wangu Textile, the transformation to a brand owner was rather smooth and successful. Wangu supplied custom-made fabrics for some leading luxury brands, including Dunhill, Celina, and Chanel. It also weaved scarves as an OEM for brands such as Pierre Cardin. In addition to these, Wangu produced scarves, curtains, bed textiles, and household decorative textiles under its own brand "Mantani," which targets the high-end markets such as Japan and Europe. Wangu celebrated its tenth anniversary in 2007, and its goal for the next 10 years is to strengthen its own brand. "We focused on manufacturing in the first 10 years and we're going to focus on marketing for the next 10 years," says Yan Han, Wangu President.

Wangu has always attached great importance to R&D. At the launch of its factory, it had only six sets of machinery but at least seven designers on board, twice or triple the number of designers in competing factories. These designers were able to develop more than 40 new patterns every week, giving Wangu a competitive edge in the establishment of its own brand. In the past two years, Wangu has gradually begun marketing its brands through magazine advertisements in Japan and Europe. In addition, Wangu reached a deal with a company to market and sell its products in the Japanese market. This is how Wangu products could be found on the shelves of some of Japan's most exclusive shopping centers, making it the first Chinese brand with such a high profile. With its success in Europe and Japan, Wangu plans to explore the domestic market with the launch of its first branded shop in Hangzhou in the near future.

Transformation from Sales-Oriented Strategy to Marketing-Oriented Strategy

By 2000, Wang Yaohai's Opple Lighting had grown significantly, with several dozen employees and an annual sales revenue of RMB 10 million. Wang then decided to take some courses on business management, and he was quite impressed with a marketing course taught by Professor Bao Zhen from the Renmin University of China.[5] Wang paid handsomely for Bao's marketing consultancy services and it proved to be a wise investment. Opple's sales revenue jumped to over RMB 100 million in 2001 and over RMB 200 million in 2002.

In 2003, Wang made another big investment in brand building. He hired the "founder of CIS" (a Japanese consulting company) to provide his consulting service. This, however, turned out to be a failure. "In the following two to three years, we had to make adjustments to rectify the effects brought by this project," Wang says. CIS provided consulting services to many Chinese enterprises in the consumer electronics industry in the 1990s. It advocated a strategy of increasing market share through advertising and price cuts. "In retrospect, this move did serious harm to Opple," says Wang. Opple's sales revenue continued to increase in 2003, but there was no coinciding rise in profits. Most household lighting fixture manufacturers in China were grouped in the low-end market. They based their competition on the lowest prices possible, sometimes at the cost of the quality of raw materials. Opple had targeted the mid-range market with better quality products, which would inevitably affect its profit margin if they cut prices without lowering the quality of raw materials and products.

What's more, a sales-oriented strategy leads people to focus solely on the sales data. Market and branding are neglected. In 2004, Opple hired PricewaterhouseCoopers to design a performance assessment system. Unfortunately, the system only made the situation worse as the assessment system was completely based on sales. There were often sharp sales increases at the end of the month or end of the year which led to the company being out of stock, but if production was increased to meet sales demands, it could result in overstocked inventory in the following month.

To become a product- and market-oriented enterprise, Wang realized, Opple must change the current sales-oriented model. Opple began to shift its budget focus from sales to marketing. Market research, product R&D, and product development team building were given high priority to better meet current market demands as well as lead and shape future market trends. Domestic household lighting fixture manufacturers usually focus on industrial design in their R&D. As designs are easily copied, it is hard to keep competitive on this aspect. Opple focused its R&D on the quality of light, which was harder to copy. Its products serve both decorative and functional purposes, satisfying customer demand for good design as well as high-quality lighting. The effort to shift focus from sales to marketing has paid off well. Opple has become an established name brand in China's lighting industry. It was selected one of the 500 most valuable brands in China, and its sales revenues surpassed RMB 1 billion in 2006.

Transformation from Single Product Line to Multi-Product Lines

In 1997, due to China's tax rebate reduction on foreign trade a year earlier and the Asian financial crisis, Tony Zhang found the parent company that he worked for on the verge of bankruptcy, despite the fact that the Shanghai branch that he headed accounted for 70% to 80% of the parent's total profits. Given his ability and the company's difficulty, he bought the state-owned trading company for between

RMB 4 and RMB 5 million. Tony's Group then began to shift from foreign trade on chemicals and non-ferrous metal to domestic trade.

Tony is quite sociable and enjoys entertaining and making friends, often inviting clients and friends for lunch or dinner. At that time, there were few Sichuan restaurants in Shanghai so Tony decided to open one for the convenience of entertaining friends. The restaurant was an unexpected success, even though it was not located in the most desirable area and was relatively small at 150 square meters. Within a month, there were long lines of customers waiting for a seat. And soon, its reputation attracted pop stars and celebrities from Hong Kong, adding to its popularity. Tony later expanded the restaurant to the upper floor of the building and increased its space to 400 square meters. Tony believes the success of the restaurant was due to two factors: it offered authentic and delicious Sichuan flavors, and the decor was stylish and unique. Not much attention was paid to the dining environment in Chinese restaurants at that time, but young people in Shanghai were very responsive to new trendy things.

Tony has continued to enter into a variety of businesses. He bought a 20% stake in a deal to purchase a phosphorite mine that had about 200 million tons of phosphorite reserves. This could be integrated with his non-ferrous metal trade business. When the Shanghai Yangshan Deep Water Port was still in the planning stages in 2002, Tony bought about 70,000 square meters of land in the area. Now the value of this plot has soared due to its prime location adjacent to a major transportation route, and numerous logistics companies have contacted him for possible cooperation. Tony plans to select a major and well-established logistics company as a partner to jointly set up a logistics and warehouse company.

In 2005, Tony bought over one million square meters of land in Nanhui with an eye to build a farm and grow greenhouse vegetables. The idea was to combine agricultural tourism with high-value vegetable production—a new model for the agricultural business. The vegetables could be nicely packaged and sold in Shanghai. Freshness and safety were the selling points. The government had also listed agriculture as an eligible business for subsidies. Tony received a government subsidy of RMB 10 million in addition to government policy support.

As there are not many relevant tie-ins among Tony's different businesses, his original business continued to decline while the newly developed restaurant business provided a solid growth point for the group. And the acquisition of land and natural resources provided opportunities for sustainable development.

Building Organizational Capability

Many private enterprises didn't even have a formal business plan at the initial founding period, let alone a strategy. However, with the growth of the enterprises, the entrepreneurs began to devote more effort to building their core competitiveness and transforming their business models. They gradually built up their organizational capability through employee recruitment and training (to increase employees' competency), corporate culture, talent retention, and performance management (to change employees' mindset).

Recruitment

At the initial founding period, it was hard for POEs to recruit talented people, since they were not well-known companies and could not afford to pay attractive salaries. They could only get those who would accept low salaries and were willing to grow with the enterprise. Cao Xianglai of Zhongxin Chemical says, "Most of my first group of employees didn't have a very good educational background. But they were willing to work with me on the business." Chang Xuehong of Shanghai Compass Global Freight Company admits cost control was the first priority at the initial founding stage, so salaries were low.

With business growth, enterprises began to change their requirements for new recruits. Chang says they are now taking a cost–benefit approach to setting salary levels for new hires. "I don't care how much they ask. The key factor is how much value they can bring to the company." Cao Xianglai took the same approach. He began to change his recruitment requirements in 2002. Firstly, candidates must have an education in chemistry. Secondly, the candidate must be fluent in English as Zhongxin Chemical is involved in the foreign trade of chemicals.

The emphasis on new employees' professional skills can also be seen in Bridge HR's recruitment. "All new recruits must have an education background in human resource management or business administration," CEO Hou Zhengyu says. "Mid- and top-level managers must have worked in HR management." In addition, Bridge HR gave high priority to employees' recognition of its corporate culture, which puts the customer first, the investor second, and the career development of employees third.

Aiminger Leather Goods also stressed employees' recognition of its corporate culture and identification with team values. All new employees, whether they were managers or salespeople, were required to take a one-month training course at the production line to gain first-hand experience in shoemaking. There are a total of 106 steps in Aiminger's shoemaking workflow. This not only gave employees first-hand knowledge of the procedures that go into making a shoe, but also helps with the problem-solving process, says Liu Qiongying. Managers were better able to identify the source of problems in production, and therefore were quicker to offer effective solutions. Another aim of this exercise is to give managers a respect for those on the production line, making for easier communication between managers and workers. As a matter of fact, the most important criterion in Aiminger's recruitment was the recognition of team values and the ability to integrate into the team.

Training

In the course of Chinese POEs' growth and development, some of them turned to consulting companies for services and employee training. In the early period of China's reform and opening up, consulting services were new to domestic companies. Only foreign companies or joint ventures would seek this kind of service. Now the situation has changed. And as a matter of fact, some domestic POEs seem to be very concerned with outsourcing consultant services. One example is Opple Lighting. Following are the consultant services they have outsourced:

- Consulting service on marketing from Professor Ban Zheng from the Renmin University of China, 2001
- CIS service from a well-known Japanese company, 2004
- Performance evaluation service from PricewaterhouseCoopers, 2004
- ERP from SAP, 2005

All of the services listed involved steep fees and they did not always end with desired results. However, Opple remains a firm believer in this kind of "book smarts."

Hightex Company of Hangzhou outsourced training programs for its employees from consulting companies. What is more, Hightex's president Lu Wenlong requires his top managers to earn their MBAs at Zhejiang University[6] after he himself took an MBA course there and found it very useful. When he returned to the company to communicate the new concepts, he found that his management team did not fully comprehend them and worried that it would hamper their implementation. So Lu became determined to have his top managers get an MBA education.

Aiminger Leather Goods provided various training for managers. The training was not only on professional skills such as cost control, performance evaluation, and leadership development. It also included moral cultivation and character building. Liu Qiongying believed these benefit the cultivation of a team-building spirit. Job dissatisfaction mostly arises when one employee compares himself or herself with others. If one suspects that another, who contributed less, was better paid, he or she would lose morale. Moral cultivation and character building were aimed to get rid of this "comparison mentality," and make every member of the team realize that although individual contributions may vary on different projects, it all evens out in the end.

Corporate Culture

The saying that "Corporate culture is the boss's culture" is to a large extent reality in many Chinese POEs. Corporate culture in these POEs often reflects the philosophy and personality of the boss. Shanghai Original Enterprise puts people first as the core value of its corporate culture. "We believe in cultivating the moral integrity of our people. We think that's the foundation of good performance. In the same approach, we put product quality as a top priority," says Hou Hailiang, founder of Original Enterprise.

This corporate culture aligns with Hou's personal beliefs. He tells each new employee: "We provide equal opportunity to every employee. The company is a platform for everybody to show his or her talent. You may not receive a very high pay when you join and the facilities may not be the best, but the greatest advantage we can offer is plenty of opportunities." This is Hou's effort to give back the learning and opportunities he received when he worked at a state-owned cable factory.

The cheerful and gregarious Wang Zhi, General Manager of SPN Technology, wanted to create a "generally accepted" culture. "I hope to create a pleasant working environment where there is no competition among colleagues. I'd rather have my staff feel relaxed, although this may lead to certain inefficiencies," Wang says. "I tell them to compete with themselves. For example, I'd ask them to compare their own performance and the bonus they earned last year with what they expect to receive this year."

For Tony's Group Chairman Tony Zhang brotherhood is an essential moral value. His work experience as a grassroots government official made him realize the importance of respecting grassroots people. His hospitality as a host in Shanghai extended to every visiting friend from his home province of Sichuan, without distinction as to their careers or social status. Tony took the same approach in building his corporate culture. He tried to create a culture of love "with some humanistic content." "We have strict company rules that are firmly adhered to. In the mean time, we take good care of our employees. When they experience personal difficulties, we will try our best to help them out," he says.

Shanghai Xhan Yang Chemical Company is the best example of "Corporate culture is the boss's culture." CEO Cheryl Chen spent several years of her childhood in China's autonomous region among ethnic Koreans. Most of her work experience was within a Korean environment, including a job in Korea and another job in a Korean company's Shanghai office. The prolonged exposure to Korean culture made its impact on Cheryl. When she and her sister founded their own company, she tried to introduce the Korean culture into it. For example, upon entering the office, all employees were required to take off their shoes and put on slippers supplied by the company. Some employees resisted this influence, and Cheryl went so far as to send certain key employees to Korea to study and train. "They would start learning it once they realize it is something better. People are naturally inclined to learn and pursue something good," Cheryl says.

Compensation, Performance Evaluation, and Talent Retention

As to issues of employee compensation, talent retention, and incentives, some of the practices that are common among the private enterprises we investigated include: compensation levels are at the upper-middle end of the industry; employee turnover is generally low; bonuses are the main incentive, stock options and grants are rare; and housing benefits are used to retain key talent.

President of Merryland Real Estate Development Gao Qi says the company's salaries were at the upper-middle level within the industry, and the low employee turnover was mainly due to two factors: the company has a promising future and a pleasant work environment without much annoying office politics. "You may make mistakes. You may voice complaints. But it's all about work. We never get personal," Gao says. Similar to Merryland, KeyPoint Controls also had upper-middle level compensation and a rather stable team, especially the key team members. KeyPoint President Liang Qihua says he firmly believes that the most important asset of an enterprise is its people. KeyPoint made every effort to create a pleasant working environment, including offering various benefits, annual pay rises, and an employee career development plan, among others.

Zhongxin Chemical uses the most common means of compensation. Its front-line staff's compensation is composed of a base salary and a performance-linked bonus. The management team receives a year-end bonus that is also linked to performance. These have proven effective as employee turnover is low. Many people working there today are the same people who joined in the early days of the company. After moving the headquarters from Hainan to Shanghai, however, Cao Xianglai found that conditions were different and the company had to change its compensation approach. In the 1980s, Hainan attracted a large number of talent from across the country and Cao supplied apartments and a canteen for employees, hoping to create a family-like atmosphere. In Shanghai, however, such benefits were not necessary as many of the employees were from the area. "Employees in Shanghai are more concerned about salary levels," Cao says.

Aiminger Leather Goods uses corporate culture and performance evaluation to retain employees. Its corporate culture aims to build employees' attachment to Aiminger, including professional skills training, courses on moral cultivation and character building, and well-organized leisure activities. Aiminger's management team has an incentive to maintain the company's 40% annual growth rate as they receive bonuses based on performance; additionally, they receive a 5% to 10% salary increase if they continue working for the company. This is a key factor for the stability of the management team.

SPN Technology General Manager Wang Zhi believes SPN's future and brand name within the industry are important to employee retention, but even more important is his reputation for tolerance and generosity. "In their eyes, I'm the kind of boss who doesn't haggle over trivial things. I don't make a big issue over small accidental mistakes," Wang says. "We also make it a rule that any employee can borrow money from the company to buy his or her own apartment and I never ask when they can repay the money." This has in fact proved to be an excellent way to retain employees. People realize that as long as they stayed at the company, they did not have to repay the loan, but as soon as they left they needed to return it in full.

Wangu Textile also uses housing benefits to retain its key talent. The company was fortunate enough to buy a number of apartments before real estate prices skyrocketed. It now offers key personnel the opportunity to buy the units at the original price. Wangu also offers opportunities to study and train overseas as an incentive for the key talents to stay with the company.

Bridge HR has been able to recruit top managers, some of whom have even worked at international companies as HR directors. Why did these people leave their attractive salaries and stable jobs for a local startup? Hou Zhengyu believes that in addition to money, career development and personal attachments were important factors. For many Chinese managers working for foreign enterprises, they come across a so-called glass ceiling. At Bridge HR, says Hou, the room for development is much more expansive.

As chairman, Hou also nurtures personal attachments with his newly recruited senior managers. "If I can learn from him, I'll treat him as a teacher. If he performs his duties well, I'll treat him as a friend. If he can't contribute much to the company, I'll treat him as a guest," Hou says. Bridge HR is also one of the only few Chinese private enterprises that offers company shares to its top managers, who can expect additional shares for excellent performance.

Speedup's Michael Ma combines economic benefits with persuasive logic to retain his talent. Almost all the middle and top managers at Speedup joined during its founding period. They are in their career development prime and have gained a certain amount of skills and experience, and should be job-hopping as is the norm for this age group. Yet according to Michael, Speedup has the lowest employee turnover in the industry. He says there are three reasons: compensation is on par with other companies in the industry, employees sign a three-year contract instead of a one-year contract, and he uses persuasion to retain key personnel.

For example, he uses the following logic on his employees: "If your salary is RMB 50,000 at Speedup and a competitor offers you RMB 150,000, they're buying your resources and experience. Once you join them, they take over your resources and experience and you are no longer worth RMB 150,000. If you can earn RMB 150,000 outside the industry, then that is your real value. If this is the case, and I can't increase your salary to RMB 150,000, you may as well leave."

Another reason that employees have stayed on at Speedup is the decision to turn the six departments into individual profit centers and to link profits to their compensation. "If the six profit centers do well, the heads' compensation can go well above RMB 150,000. They could get RMB 400,000 to RMB 500,000 if their profit reaches RMB 3,000,000," Ma says. "They would remain employees if they went to other companies. Here, they could become small bosses."

Among the enterprises we investigated, Tony's Group spends the most money on attracting and retaining talent. In addition to providing housing and a car (plus gas and insurance), Tony's Group gives shares worth as much as RMB 1 million to top managers. To keep these people closely tied to the company, Tony's Group requires them to invest RMB 2.8 million for two years in the company's shares, after which time they will be granted shares worth about RMB 4 million that can be cashed in after five years. Compensation comes from two sources: base pay and performance-related pay. Top managers derive most of their annual income from profit distribution, while compensation for other employees is divided into 70% base pay and 30% performance-related pay.

On the issues of recruitment, compensation, incentive schemes, and employee turnover, Hightex president Lu Wenlong has a unique view and practice. When interviewing candidates for top and middle management posts, Lu prefers those who have their own homes and cars. "If you're over 30 years old and you don't have your own home, I'd think you don't have the ability and the sense of responsibility to manage your own life well. If that's the case, how could you have the ability and sense of responsibility to manage my enterprise?"

With regard to incentive schemes, Lu believes they should keep pace with changing situations. "Bonuses used to be an effective incentive. It's become less effective as the living standard in China continues to grow. So the incentive scheme should include career promotion in addition to financial rewards," he explains. Lu also believes that creative talent begins to fade after five to eight years at a company; work becomes routine and people may not be able to contribute much. Enterprises should, therefore, seek a continuous injection of fresh blood to maintain its innovative contributions.

Lu notes that Hightex's compensation is very high compared with the industry standard. As a manufacturing enterprise, Hightex's blue-collar technical workers are given a very important role and can earn more than white-collar workers in the company. As for employee benefits, Hightex lends money to employees to pay the down payment for their home purchases. And like other companies, Hightex also uses performance-based pay, but its formula was designed by the whole management team where the rewards were not too high or low, meaning they were obtainable if workers put in the extra effort.

What is unique to Hightex's management approach is its salary scheme. Lu calls it "one enterprise, many systems." Every employee is given the opportunity to select his or her terms of payment. Most prefer a base salary and performance-based bonus. Because it is difficult to recruit good talent to the textiles field, Lu says that a flexible salary scheme is aimed at attracting the most-needed talent. "Our profits were a little affected by the negotiable salary arrangement but it's all right with me. I can accept it," Lu says.

Confidentiality is very important to this salary system as comparisons could result in discontent, Lu admits. Bonuses are also negotiable. Some prefer bonuses based on individual performance while others prefer bonuses based on team performance. "Evaluations must be designed to take into account both individual and team contributions," he says. Even the working hours in the factory are set through negotiation. Some workers prefer the three-shifts arrangement and others prefer the two-shifts arrangement. Workers choose which work group to join and each work group sets its own schedule.

Chinese POEs show great flexibility in retaining and compensating their talent. It is also notable that many of them use corporate culture and emotional attachment to retain employees.

Corporate Governance

In this section, we will discuss Chinese POEs' corporate governance, including their ownership structure and agency problems.

Ownership Structure: Joint Venture vs. Wholly Owned Enterprise

On the issue of joint venture or wholly owned enterprise, the enterprises we looked at can be put into three categories:

- Enterprises that remain wholly owned
- Shift from joint ventures to wholly owned enterprises
- From one joint venture to another to secure necessary resources for further expansion

Enterprises that Remain Wholly Owned   Enterprises in this category include those founded by Cao Xianglai, Liu Qiongying, Tony Zhang, Han Yan, and Lu Wenlong. From their beginnings to their development, these enterprises have been and continue to be wholly owned. We also put enterprises co-founded with family members in this category. They include those founded by Lou Xiuhua and her husband, Wang Yaohai and his wife, as well as Cheryl Chen and her sister.

Of the 20 enterprises featured, one-third fall into the wholly owned category. The biggest advantage is that the entrepreneur can determine the company's development path based on personal philosophy or vision. The disadvantage is that the company's development may suffer from a lack of resources.

Shift from Joint Ventures to Wholly Owned Enterprises   In many respects, a joint venture is like a marriage. Understanding is essential, as are mutual trust, shared values, and goals between partners. Many of those who we interviewed in this category, however, elected to enter joint ventures for financial reasons and did not have any understanding or shared values and goals between them. This became a problem when the joint venture reached a certain stage of development. If the situation worsened and was combined with a lack of mutual trust, the joint venture was doomed to break up.

General Manager of Compass Global Freight Chang Xuehong faced these problems in the early stages of his joint venture with friends. He and his four friends each invested RMB 100,000 into the joint venture in 2000, but after six months one partner needed to withdraw from the investment so Chang bought out his share. By early 2001, another partner withdrew and Chang took over those shares as well.

The company then faced serious cash flow problems due to slow business, so Chang struck up a cooperative deal with an SOE, but that did not go well and the SOE subsequently failed to fulfill its part of the deal. By early 2003, Chang decided to end the cooperation and continue alone. He says, "Cargo transport is different from a capital-intensive industry where capital investment is the most important asset and the relative power depends on the amount of individual investment. Cargo transport is a service business. It's hard to define each partner's contribution. If decisions were made only on the basis of percentage of ownership, there would be a lot of internal problems."

KeyPoint Controls entered two joint ventures, and both broke up due to the lack of mutual trust and shared values. KeyPoint was established in 2000 by four parties, each of whom contributed RMB 200,000 and owned a 25% share. In its first year, the company earned RMB 1 million. "Once two of the shareholders saw how quickly profits were coming, they raised some issues," says Liang Qihua, who was the only partner who took part in the management of the company. A lack of trust became a major issue and, in 2002, the two partners broke up the partnership and sold their shares to Liang.

Later in 2004, Liang bought a 37% stake in a manufacturing company for RMB 1 million. Two other investors respectively held 33% and 30% shares. As the biggest shareholder, Liang was elected chairman and general manager of the enterprise. To solve cash flow problems, Liang invested an additional RMB 3 million into the enterprise, and by the end of 2005 the two partners "raised some new issues" about the joint venture. The first issue was about their mistrust of Liang, and the second was about profit distribution. They wanted more of the profit while Liang wanted to reinvest it into the business. To break the impasse, Liang proposed buying out the two investors or having them buy him out, thinking that they were financially unable to buy him out and having no intention of selling his shares. However, one of the investors got capital support from his wealthy girlfriend, and Liang was eventually bought out for RMB 1.6 million.

The break-up of SPN Technology's original partners was mainly due to the lack of shared values on management philosophy. Wang Zhi founded SPN in 2001 with two other investors; one was a colleague at a Taiwanese company where they both worked, and the other was a former supplier. They did not sign a contract detailing their various shareholdings; instead their partnership was based on a division of labor. Wang was the general manager in charge of the automotive control equipment market. His former colleague was in charge of the engineering machinery market.

After only three months, the two other investors became engaged in a serious conflict and Wang had to choose between them. He asked the former supplier to leave the partnership as the other investor was very young without much work experience. "If I let him go, he'd be jobless," Wang recalls thinking. But the difficulties did not end. Wang realized he did not share the same values with the remaining partner. First, Wang sought to build customer relations while his partner considered SPN's technology the biggest priority and did not approve of Wang's efforts. Secondly, their management styles were radically different. The partner managed employees with aggression and intimidation while Wang was kind and lenient. Many talented people left the company because of clashes with the young partner. "Our business requires a high level of professional skill and it takes about two years to train new employees. We spent so much time and effort to train them for naught," says Wang.

By the end of 2003, Wang was desperate to break up the joint venture. The company was losing money at that time and the only asset that they could split was the client list. "You know what was in my mind? I just wanted to break from him even if it meant that I was left with nothing more than a shell," he says. At last, the partner left, taking some clients and eventually becoming SPN's competitor.

As earlier mentioned, Original Enterprise received the most bank loans of the companies we feature, due partly to the capital-intensive nature of the company. Hou Hailiang had a number of partners in the course of Original Enterprise's growth, many of them creditors turned shareholders. From 2001 to 2002, an investor joined Original with several million yuan. The money was initially given as a loan and later turned into an investment. In 2002, a state-owned commercial group joined as a main shareholder with several million yuan, half of which was investment, half of which was a loan.

At the same time, a former investor decided to withdraw his investment because of a lack of immediate return. He proposed that Hou sell the company so he could collect his share, but Hou refused. "Original Enterprise was my enterprise. I couldn't sell it— it was still developing. Business was growing," Hou says. He had to repurchase the investor's shares with twice his initial investment. At the end of 2003, Original began negotiating with Italian company Solvay Padanaplast about the possibility of a joint venture, and reached a deal the following year. Padanaplast Original Advanced Compounds (Shanghai) Company was established, with each side holding a 50% share. Original was in charge of the operations, and board meetings were held each season.

A major difference between the two companies' styles was that Padanaplast was process-based while Original was flexible and responsive to market needs. Product approach best illustrates these differences. "A customer once said, 'I know Padanaplast has good-quality products, the raw materials are always of excellent quality, but other manufacturers offer lower prices. I care about price, I don't care if you use lower quality material,'" Hou recalls. However, this was an issue Padanaplast did not agree with. It insisted on high quality and high prices, which seriously affected their sales. Meanwhile, prices for oil and copper increased, further boosting their costs. Original was being squeezed on both sides, and Hou began to rethink the partnership with Padanaplast.

From One Joint Venture to Another to Secure Necessary Resources for Further Expansion   KeyPoint Technology and Original Enterprise are two examples of companies that exchanged one joint venture for another. After two failed joint ventures, KeyPoint President Liang Qihua introduced two new investors—one was a supplier and the other was a customer. The greatest advantage of this kind of cooperation was that it was conducive to the maximization of the value creation due to the shared goals and common interests among concerned parties as well as the integration of the industry chain. "In addition to that, our partners have rich industry experience which helps us a lot," Liang says. Nevertheless, Liang learned some lessons from his past ventures. "I realized from the last experience the importance of profit distribution to shareholders. This joint venture distributes at least 20% of its profit," Liang says.

As Original Enterprise's joint venture with the Italian company Padanaplast was pressured from both upstream suppliers and downstream customers, Hou Hailiang adjusted his development strategy. He says, "In the past, when I couldn't reach consensus with partners I would try my best to repurchase his shares and carry out things my way. Now, so long as it is conducive to the healthy development of the company and the continuous growth of our business, I can temporarily make concessions."

Hou seemed to have no choice when he began seeking joint venture partners along the industry chain. A potential partner was a cable manufacturer but a joint venture with this partner would move Original Enterprise downstream the industry chain and turn it from a cable material manufacturer into a cable manufacturer. Hou knew that Original Enterprise did not have much bargaining power in a feasible joint venture whether it chose to move upstream by cooperating with petrochemical manufacturers or moving downstream. "The process of integration will be very difficult," he says.

"Insiders" vs. Professional Managers

At the founding stage of an enterprise, insiders such as relatives are the most reliable people available, seeing the company has yet to establish its reputation in the industry to attract valuable employees or afford expensive professional managers. More importantly, a private enterprise at this stage needs wholly devoted and hardworking people who share a common goal. As a company grows, however, many of our entrepreneurs have found that insiders lack the right mindset and skills needed to help the company develop. Professional managers are needed, but if the insiders stay on after such managers come aboard, conflicts may arise. In this case, some entrepreneurs elect to let go of the insiders, especially if it is their spouse. Others choose to play the role of an intermediary between the two groups.

Insiders are Reliable   The catering portion of Tony's Group was initially run by family members, says Tony Zhang. "At the founding stage, loyalty and shared goals are very important, which are the biggest advantages of family management. Everyone is completely devoted to the business without caring about working overtime or compensation," he says. Among the enterprises we studied, Tony's was the one with the most number of insiders. They include his wife, brothers, sisters, and other relatives. "The biggest difference between insiders and outside employees is the sense of responsibility and initiative," he says.

Aiminger Leather Goods hired many professional managers. "The most important criteria for hiring professionals is their ability," says Liu Qiongying, who has her husband in charge of procurement. It seems that insiders are more reliable in key positions.

Those directly in control of financial management must be reliable, says Michael Ma of Speedup Automobile Racing Club. Although his companies are run by professional managers, his wife is the Chief Financial Officer of Speedup and his sister is the Chief Financial Officer of Shanghai Heaven Racing Company. Ma notes that absolute control over financial issues is typical in his hometown of Wenzhou. "Where there is power, there is the abuse of power. To avoid this, I think, financial management must be in the hands of insiders."

Professional Managers Are Professional   Tony found that once success occurs, the mindset of insiders changes. "They [the insiders] have all bought houses and cars and their motivation shifts. Meanwhile, their knowledge and skills become dated," he says. The eventual reduced profit margins prompted Tony's Group to diversify from its initial trading business and the transformation was a big challenge. There was little relevance between the original business and the new ones, and much more sophisticated management skills were required. "Take the catering business for example; competitors today are completely different from when Tony's Restaurant was first opened. Some have substantial backing from real estate companies or venture capitalists and others are associated with Hong Kong's pop stars. They have enough money to hire excellent managers. If we continued to completely rely on insiders, we'd have no chance of survival," Tony explains. Although two professional managers were hired, one who studied hospitality management in Britain and the other a CEIBS EMBA holder, Tony's wife remains a board director of the restaurant.

In the course of Eitong Air Express's development from a "husband-and-wife shop" with two to three employees to an international cargo transport company that operates in over 300 cities worldwide, Lou Xiuhua saw the importance of professional management. She hired a fellow CEIBS graduate with an EMBA as the general manager, a post that was held by her husband. "The classmate has rich top-level management experience in both SOEs and POEs," Lou says. Her husband now heads channel development and Lou praises his skills in that post. Lou's management philosophy is as follows: let the proper people hold the proper positions and make full use of their respective capabilities.

As KeyPoint Controls acted as an agent, its key personnel were undoubtedly the sales managers. Liang Qihua himself was the top sales manager in the early days of the company, but as it expanded, KeyPoint hired professional sales managers. These managers were given KeyPoint shares, which could be kept even if they chose to leave the company.

Under the Same Roof   "Before bringing in professionals, you need to consider the possibility of conflicts arising between them and the insiders. If you take the side of the insiders, the professionals will leave. A failure to solve this issue could lead to major problems in the future," says Tony Zhang.

The introduction of professional managers into a family-run enterprise is to increase the management level of the enterprise. The newly recruited managers would naturally put forward some new measures which might affect the established interests of the insiders. When this is combined with abrupt changes in management style, insiders will likely harbor grievances against the newcomers.

Soon after the two professional managers with overseas educational background joined Tony's Restaurant, they proposed a series of initiatives on training and standards to improve service, but if the proposals were adopted there would be a sharp increase in cost without a quick return. Tony's wife, who is a board director, opposed the proposals on the grounds of cost, but Tony agreed with the managers. He knew that the restaurant would face an increasingly difficult situation against its competitors if the proposed measures were not adopted. He also had to justify the cost of hiring the managers as well. "I had to mediate between the two sides. I needed to work out a situation between the insiders' management philosophy and the outsiders' proposals," Tony says.

He came up with a compromise acceptable to both sides and they experimented with the proposals in two of Tony's Sichuan-Flavor Restaurants. Reforms on organizational structure were carried out, management process was established, and various trainings were conducted. The two restaurants directly reported the results to Tony. "It's like growing a new variety of plant in an experimental field. If it yielded good results, the insiders would be convinced. And you could extend it to all restaurants. If it failed, it wouldn't do any serious harm," Tony says.

We also found in our research that when conflicts arose between the insiders and professional managers, entrepreneurs tend to intentionally take the side of the outsiders even though it was emotionally difficult to do so—much as it was for Tony. This was also the case for Merryland Real Estate Development. President Gao Qi hired her brother, but found that his strong personality and sense of responsibility was at odds with the company's management. "My brother voiced opinions where his voice shouldn't be heard, and took responsibilities that were not part of his job. The top managers felt their authority and power were threatened. How would you expect them to carry out their responsibilities?" she notes. On issues that Gao thought might hurt the initiative of the managers, Gao always openly refused to take sides with her brother, even though he was able to root out some problems and saved the company thousands of RMB. Gao also insisted that her brother report to his superior instead of bypassing him and going directly to her. However, her brother could not appreciate her intentions and often complained about her taking sides with "outsiders." He has even complained to their parents. This misunderstanding with her brother remains a difficulty for Gao.

To solve the conflict between insiders and outsiders, Jason Zhang, General Manager of Dynaforge Tools & Hardware Company, chose to let the insider go. His wife, who helped found the company, took maternity leave when she gave birth. During her absence, Jason hired new employees. "When she returned, she quarreled with some of them," Jason recalls. He believes the problem lay in how his wife positioned herself in the company; she thought she held a special position as the boss's wife and often voiced opinions different from Jason's in the company. The employees were torn between the two. "I mostly sided with the employees," Jason says. But that did not resolve the conflict between her and the employees. A few left the company, and Jason admits that a third of the reason was because of his wife. He felt he had no choice but to relegate his wife and her duties to their home.

According to Hou Hailiang of Original Enterprise, even if there is no conflict between insiders and professional managers or employees, the special status of insiders still places them in an embarrassing position. "Even if the insiders behave the same as the others, they still look different," Hou says. His wife used to be in charge of HR in the company and his brother was in charge of purchasing and engineering. Hou eventually persuaded both of them to leave.

"When the enterprise reached a certain scale, it's best to let the insiders go as eventually there will be conflict between them and employees," Jason says. "For the sake of long-term interest in the enterprise, you can't ask your employees to sacrifice their interests to avoid conflict. However, the greatest advantage of insiders is that he or she can make sacrifices for the enterprise."

Insiders: The Balance between Work and Family   The presence of insiders in the management of an enterprise might not only cause conflict but also lead to disagreement between the insiders and the entrepreneur. Such a disagreement can sometimes affect the family life, especially when it involves a husband and wife. To maintain the balance between work and family, many of the entrepreneurs we studied chose to keep their spouses out from the beginning or to let the insiders go very early.

Wang Zhi of SPN Technology never had to worry about balancing work with family. He did not even consider involving his wife in the business. "I don't like my family being involved in my business," Wang says, adding that the situation suited his wife. In the seven years of SPN's operations, Wang's wife has visited the office twice and both visits were on Saturday. "The only company employee who has met my wife is the driver," he notes.

Gao Qi of Merryland Real Estate also did not involve her spouse in the business but experienced problems nonetheless. A disagreement arose when Gao and her husband disagreed on the amount of discount a friend of his should receive in the purchase of a Merryland property. "It wasn't the matter of the discount, the point is he disregarded the company's rules," says Gao. "Merryland is not a husband-and-wife company in which you can do whatever you like. Merryland's achievement is the result of every employee's devoted efforts. You must respect them." Gao says jokingly that if her husband became interested in running an enterprise, she would definitely let him do it alone.

Cao Xianglai of Hainan Zhongxin Chemical started his enterprise with his wife, but let her leave in the early stages of the company. "It's because of my character. I'm rather insistent and stubborn. If she stayed in the company, we would have had many arguments. It would have affected our relationship," he says.

With regard to balancing work and family, Wang Yaohai of Opple held a different view from most of those we interviewed. He prefers to run the company with his wife. Wang's wife made great contributions to Opple's development. "Actually, we have different management styles. It's normal to have arguments, which can lead to solutions. An enterprise shouldn't just follow one voice. Different voices should be heard. Especially during Opple's transformation, discussions and arguments are needed on a lot of issues." Wang also admits, however, that arguments with his wife could be very intense, making him concerned whether it would harm their relationship.

President of Hightex Lu Wenlong was an example of someone who strongly opposes mixing family and business. He believes a good enterprise must practice the concepts of modern corporate management. "Within an enterprise, all activities can be considered corporate behavior," he says. In response to requests that insiders be involved in his business, Lu had a unique solution. His first enterprise was Hualong Textiles Decoration, which he founded in 1994 on his own. Not long afterward, the company began making a large profit. In 1999, Lu's two brothers, who were both high school teachers, expressed a wish to join him in the business; instead, Lu handed them the control of the business and started a new enterprise, which eventually became Hightex.

Bottlenecks

Bottleneck 1: Talented People

When asked what was the biggest bottleneck in their current stage of development, the answer of almost all the interviewees was "people." In the last chapter, we discussed the development of Chinese private enterprises: trader, manufacturer, and technology developer. The enterprises of most of the entrepreneurs we interviewed are in transition from one stage to another. In the early period of development, most of the enterprises were sales-oriented. The founder of the enterprise was often the key and best salesperson. They focused most of their time and effort on customer and market development. In their eyes, it was neither possible nor necessary to spend time and effort on issues such as corporate culture and employee training.

When enterprises reach a certain scale and need to transform to maintain profit margins, the leaders have come to realize that the most essential factor is that they must have core competencies. How does one build core competencies? Where does one find competent employees to support it? The problems stem from the fact that current employees cannot meet the requirements at this stage, recruiting new ones is expensive, and retaining competent people is getting harder given the low supply and high demand for qualified, talented people.

Shortage of Talent for Specific Jobs   When the export-oriented Aiminger Leather Goods began to explore the domestic market for its products, one of the challenges it faced was the shortage of competent people. According to Liu Qiongying, the plan to develop the domestic market began in 2005. Since then, she has been looking for the appropriate people to implement the plan. So far, she has not been able to find the right people that "matched" her criteria.

The General Manager of Shanghai Speedup Automobile Racing Club, Michael Ma, says the general preoccupation with immediate monetary gains among Chinese employees makes it difficult for them to be trained as highly competent professional mechanics. His club's Volkswagen Fortune Racing Team's key maintenance staff are all German and Japanese.

Shortage of Talent across All Industries   Ma also mentions the general acute shortage of management talent in the whole car racing industry. "So far, all of our management people are internally trained and promoted," he says. The shortage of all kinds of talent does not only exist in newly emerged industries such as car racing, it has also become a major bottleneck in some traditional industries. Yan Han, President of Wangu Textile, also notes that the lack of talented people is his biggest bottleneck because so few young people today choose to enter such a traditional industry as textiles.

But the new industries do not have it any easier. According to Tong Liqun, president of Runway Technology, the greatest challenge in building an expert-run enterprise was the shortage of talent. "I'm not worried about the marketing of my products," says Tong, very confident in his judgments on market and industry trends. "My only concern is to obtain talented people to realize the product design and sell the products to the market."

The Acute Shortage of Talent for Globalized Operation   As an international trader, Hainan Zhongxin Chemical has over 500 international customers spreading across more than 70 countries. Zhongxin has offices in South Africa, South America, and Europe. It planned to open new offices in North America and the Middle East because General Manager Cao Xianglai believes globalized talent is essential to a foreign trading company such as Zhongxin, but China has an acute shortage of qualified talent. And Cao thinks the situation will not improve in the short term. "Globalized talent refers to those with global perspective, background and experience," Cao says.

Bottleneck 2: Funding

With the increasingly fierce competition and the consequent decreasing profit margins, most of the companies we feature are transforming their business models. Transformations generally require big investment. As agents or distributors, companies do not need to have sufficient fixed assets as collateral for obtaining bank loans. The lack of funding had thus become another major bottleneck in their businesses.

The Uncrossable Chasm   Especially for the trade-oriented POEs, there is a virtually uncrossable chasm between them and the bank loan. When Shanghai KeyPoint Controls began the transformation from an agent to a service provider, lack of funding became a big problem. According to KeyPoint President Liang Qihua a POE such as KeyPoint was "discriminated against" by Chinese banks, which made low valuation on the fixed assets of trading companies. The lack of collateral hampered KeyPoint's ability to secure a bank loan. It instead used letters of credit or advance payment for goods to maintain cash flow. The company's plans to build its own factory within two years will require a huge investment, however. "It's an annoying headache for me," Liang says.

General Manager of SPN Technology, Wang Zhi, says funding was his biggest problem. SPN Technology's profit mainly comes from agenting for foreign manufacturers. "The partnership with foreign manufacturers might end at any time. This is a big potential risk," Wang Zhi admits. This risk was the main reason why banks refused loans to SPN. And because the company is shifting from agent to brand owner, it must be very careful to avoid being accused by foreign partners of producing and selling products of its own, which could end valuable partnerships.

This made Wang refrain from using bank loans to finance his sensitive brand-building strategy. Instead, Wang adopted a step-by-step approach to SPN's transformation, making use of limited funding to achieve gradual progress. This was also the approach taken by the Shanghai Compass Global Freight Company. General Manager Chang Xuehong calls it an "eat-only-what-is-available" approach, meaning the pace of business expansion is determined by the amount of available funding. "If we obtained external funding support, we would have made faster progress," Wang says.

Some POEs rely on non-banking financing to support their expansion. One example is Shanghai Xhan Yang Chemical. CEO Cheryl Chen says, "A small portion of the funding was from relatives and friends, most of which was without any interest. More often we borrowed from private money lenders, who collected a rather high interest."

Changing Situations Among our sampled enterprises, Hou Hailiang's Original Enterprise Development received the largest bank loan. To some extent, this is due to the fact that Original Enterprise is a capital-intensive manufacturer.

- 1997: Hou obtained a bank loan of RMB 80,000 through the help of a friend. This was his startup capital. "Since banks at that time had rather loose control over loan approvals, it was not difficult to get loans," Hou says.
- 2001–02: An individual investor lent him several million RMB. Initially, the money was in the form of loans, then it turned into an investment.
- 2002–03: Original Enterprise was at a stage of rapid development. New lab equipment and production lines were needed, and R&D needed to be strengthened. This brought great pressure on capital. At this point, Original Enterprise introduced another major investor—a state-owned commercial group. The group invested several million RMB, 50% of which was an investment, the other 50% was a loan.

- 2003: With the help of a friend at a bank, Hou took advantage of the regulatory loopholes in loan approvals and maneuvered an "edge ball" approach to gaining bank loans. First, he obtained a loan to buy a plot of land. Then he used the land as collateral to get an additional project loan, part of which was used to build factories, and part of which was to repay loans for the land.[7] And once the factory was in full operation, he was able to pay back the loan bit by bit. In this way, he got bank loans totaling about RMB 20 million. Original Enterprise's revenue of that year was RMB 30 million.

If China's banking system had been more developed, Hou commented, Original Enterprise might have obtained more bank loans in some stages of development. Of course, Hou admits, it might not have got as many bank loans during some other stages under a more developed banking system. Hou pointed out that the key factor to secure bank loans for a private enterprise such as Original Enterprise was a promising business model. "If you were just a middleman with no fixed assets, the banks would never grant you any loans no matter what relationship you have."

Notes

1. CNCCC merged with the China National Offshore Oil Corporation in 2006.
2. The other big player at the time was Sinochem Corporation.
3. The short form for "the contracted managerial responsibility system" in China's SOEs. It was first introduced in the early 1980s as an effort to reform the SOEs. It is a special form of power-delegating and profit-sharing between the government and the SOEs. Its unique feature is that a contract is established between relevant government organs and the management of the enterprise. Under the contracting system, the party awarding the contract hands over its property to the party awarded the contract for management. The two parties reach an agreement that ensures the owner a fixed amount of profit; any profit exceeding this amount is then retained by the party awarded the contract or is shared by the two parties according to predetermined proportions.
4. Foreign investment of the joint venture was limited to a maximum 49% of the total.
5. Also known as the People's University of China.
6. One of China's best universities. It's located in Hangzhou of Zhejiang Province.
7. At that time, China's banking regulation was not well formulated. There were grey areas and loopholes in the loan-approval process. This practice is currently forbidden.

PART
IV

THREATS AND OPPORTUNITIES FOR MNCs: COMPETITION AND COOPERATION WITH CHINESE ENTREPRENEURS

CHAPTER 9

Individual Characteristics for Their Success

In terms of their size and management level, the enterprises we feature might not be considered examples of huge economic success. But when you take into consideration their current level of personal wealth as well as how far they have come from nothing to where they are today in such a short period of time, they should be seen as successful. In addition to the factors we have examined in the previous chapters, what are the individual characteristics that contribute to their success? If one's destiny is decided by one's character, what are the unique characteristics that contribute to their success?

Characteristics for Success

Our interviews and research revealed that they include the following:

- Ambition for big goals
- Breaking away from the traditional system
- Risk taking: just do it
- Diligence and hard work
- Craving for success, never surrender to defeat
- Credibility and brotherhood
- Cultivating and effectively using *guanxi*

Ambition for Big Goals

The ambition for big goals is one of the most important characteristics that differentiate a successful person. This ambition makes the person internally motivated to pursue the big goal in spite of all the hardships and difficulties. In the book *Fly Up High: A Biography of Masayoshi Son*, the author explains that Masayoshi Son's success was because of his expanding ambitions. The same can be said of our 20 entrepreneurs.

Cao Xianglai of Zhongxin Chemical, Lu Wenlong of Hangzhou Hightex, and Wang Yaohai of Opple all came from poor families and suffered the hardships and emotional stresses associated with poverty. At a very young age, they were determined to change their destiny.

Due to their poverty, Cao's family was often bullied by other villagers; his parents were once even physically beaten. Since he was a teenager, Cao told himself that he must change his destiny and help lift his family to a more affluent life. This sentiment is echoed by Lu Wenlong. "We were miserably poor and I was determined to change this. A poor family is always looked down upon by others," Lu says.

After trying his hand selling duck eggs and running a fish farm, Wang Yaohai and his wife decided to make their living in something that did not require hard physical labor and was not susceptible to severe weather. "I remember it being a time of extreme hardship; we worked everyday from dawn to night," Wang says, describing how he and his wife dug out the fish ponds themselves before a devastating typhoon killed half their stock. In the end, they were determined to change their destiny and start a business that made use of their brainpower.

"Now, I'm very happy, because I've realized my dream—I am my own boss," Cao Xianglai says. Although it is difficult to say with any certainty, chances are that Cao would not be in this happy position without having suffered hardships earlier in life.

Before starting their companies, the entrepreneurs were just like any other ordinary person. What made them different was that they were not satisfied with an ordinary life and they had the confidence that they could be more than what they were. It is this kind of ambition and self-confidence that prompted them to take the crucial first step in establishing a business.

Although Cao Xianglai was assigned to a post at a state-owned machinery factory, he resigned after less than six months and went to Hainan to pursue his riches, even though he did not know what opportunities existed or what he would do there. He did know that he did not want to waste the rest of his life in an SOE.

When Chang Xuehong of Compass Global Freight quit his job at the Shanghai Marine Bureau, he became a teacher at the Shanghai Transportation School. He was certain, however, that it was not a lifetime career move. "I'd planned to go to Shenzhen. Shanghai was just a springboard for any developments I could get started in Shenzhen," Chang says. "But the permits for visiting Shenzhen were harder to get so I had to stay in Shanghai." He spent a year studying foreign trade, then he left the school and joined a branch company of COSCO.

Lou Xiuhua of Eitong Air Express was assigned to a job at Yiwu General Textiles Factory after graduating from the Zhejiang Sci-Tech University. The hierarchy at the factory was complicated and based on seniority. There were many people waiting to reach the next rung, even some from Lou's alma mater who were in their forties. After imagining the next 20 or 30 years in such a position, Lou was determined to change course. After only a year, she quit and moved to Hangzhou.

Lu Wenlong of Hightex was the most self-confident entrepreneur among those we interviewed. "I showed great talent when I was a child. I read many classics of world literature when I was only 12 or 13 years old," Lu says. "My childhood dream was to be a physicist, not a businessman." However, to lessen the burden shouldered by his parents, Lu made the appropriate choice as a filial son—he gave up his dream and worked on various jobs such as hauling ducks, painting bikes to help the family's finances. In 1983, he quit a teaching job and found employment at a local TVE. "The only hope to become a millionaire and billionaire is through running a company. You'll never get rich by teaching," Lu, who was 23 years old at the time, told himself.

After quiting his teaching job, Lu Wenlong became a procurement clerk at a local township textile mill, and he set himself a goal: to be the director of the mill. "I was very confident at the time. I knew I was capable of the job. It wasn't a wild dream," Lu recalls. Later, through contract management, Lu actually became the director of the mill. Under his leadership, the mill's profits quadrupled. Soon after that, Lu contracted the management of another TVE.

However, being a director of TVEs was not Lu's ultimate goal. His ambition was to have an enterprise of his own. By the end of 1989, Lu resigned from the TVEs and founded his own company. Within a year, Hightex earned RMB 4 million in revenues and a profit of RMB 1 million.

Compass Global Freight's Chang Xuehong says he has been ambitious ever since high school. At that time, his classmates involuntarily associated themselves with one of the two groups of the class. Chang was the informal head of one group. The implicit rivalry between the two groups went beyond studies. It included various aspects of their school life. "Ever since then, I realized the importance of power," Chang says. "In China, the biggest power lay in the military. So I wanted to get my college education at a military university." To his disappointment, he failed the physical exam for entry.

After his first business venture failed, Chang was jobless for 10 months. He then found work at the Shanghai office of a German air cargo transport company and worked his way up from a sales clerk to import department manager and then sales manager. It was a good position in a foreign enterprise, which would have been good enough for most people, but not Chang. He considered the job a transition, and was planning to start his own company with a business model based on the German company. "I knew a lot of people who, once they started working at a foreign enterprise, got content and comfortable with life and lost their motivation and desire to take on new challenges," Chang says. In 1999, he left the German company and founded Compass Global Freight together with his friends.

A Chinese scholar, who had just returned from an overseas trip, remarked on the difference between the youth in China and those in Western countries. He said that Chinese youth are not ambitious enough. Given the thousands of years of cultural teachings on the moral values of unobtrusiveness and self-restraint, ambition is a very difficult characteristic to foster in China.

Breaking Away from the Traditional System

Quite a number of the 20 entrepreneurs have work experience with SOEs or government institutions. Their years in service range from less than a year to as long as 10 years, but all of them left because they could no longer bear the constraints of the old system.

Lou Xiuhua of Eitong Air Express was assigned to Yiwu General Textiles Factory as a lab assistant after graduating from university in 1991. Although the factory was one of the few SOEs in Yiwu making a good profit at the time, Lou was bored with the job and felt it was stifling her character. She also detested the factory's seniority-based hierarchical system, and after a year she quit.

Cheryl Chen of Xhan Yang Chemical graduated the same year as Lou Xiuhua, and was assigned to Changchun Customs. She also objected to the government agency's culture and was convinced that this was not the career path she would choose for herself. "I'm a straightforward person. I'm not good at expressing myself in a subtle way. I didn't fit in," Cheryl says. "Besides, a woman's career opportunities within customs are limited. Even if you're extremely careful and cautious, capable and politically minded, all you can expect before retirement is just a division director position. And few division directors in the customs are women." She soon quit and got a job with the Foreign Trade Company of Jilin Province.

Tony Zhang worked in the government for six years when an opportunity arose for him to move to a foreign trading company in Yibin. Although the county chief tried to persuade him to stay, he found the environment in government oppressive. "You can't say what you want. And you have to say what you don't want to say," he explains. His future in government promised him nothing more than honorable titles, which promised little material gain. So he chose to enter the world of business.

Upon graduating from university in 1984, Hou Hailiang of Original Enterprise was assigned to the state-owned Zhengzhou Cable Factory, where he worked for nine years. In 1993, tired of the bureaucracy and frustrating practices under the SOE system, he resigned despite having reached the post of deputy director of the factory's research institute. Hou echoes Tony's assessments of a traditional government system. "You can't do what you like. And you have to do what you don't like."

Underlying the rebellion against the traditional system are two leading trends in China nowadays: the decline of the SOEs and the rise of the market economy. While the former presents a certain but bleak prospect, the latter promises an uncertain but bright future. The key factor that lies behind this rebellious mindset is the pursuit of a more affluent life.

Risk Taking: Just Do It

Generally speaking, most people are risk neutral or risk averse. Only a small percentage of people are risk takers. We discovered through our interviews that risk-taking and having the courage to "just do it" are distinctive characteristics that contribute to the entrepreneurs' success. This attitude allows them to start their enterprises and make major strategic decisions.

Less than half a year after graduating from university, Cao Xianglai quit his first job with an SOE and went to Hainan. He did not know what opportunities Hainan would offer. "I didn't even think about the chance of success. I just felt I had to do it," Cao says. A similar example was Lou Xiuhua. Lou and her husband borrowed RMB 300,000 to start their business. They spent RMB 200,000 buying two automobiles, and the remaining RMB 100,000 on remodeling the office. Left with no more cash, they also felt the same determination as Cao. Lou says, "We never seriously thought about how to operate the business. All that was on our minds was to realize the dream of opening our own business."

In 1998, quality problems led to the evaporation of new orders for Aiminger Leather Goods. Desperate to maintain the business, Liu Qiongying packed a suitcase full of shoe samples and went to Russia after hearing that it was relatively easy to do business there. When asked whether she was scared about being alone in a completely foreign country, she responds, "It never crossed my mind." She returned with several modest orders, but enough to keep her company afloat and launch operations as a shoe exporter. Commenting on that crisis and her courage in coping with it, Liu says the events have become an indelible part of her memories.

There are those in our group of 20 who are more than merely risk takers, they can be described as risk seekers. An example is Gao Qi of Merryland Real Estate Development. Prior to starting her company, Gao worked in furniture retailing for five years. She knew nothing about the real estate business when she invested RMB 2 million to purchase a seven-acre plot in an industrial park in 2002. Her only knowledge was that real estate developers were investing in industrial land at that time. "It was all the money I had earned," Gao says. Her initial plan was to build plants and lease them. Given the low rents at the time, she changed her mind and left the land idle for over a year, by which time many other plants had been built in the surrounding area. Gao convinced the local government to re-zone the land use from industrial to residential for a fee of an additional RMB 8 million, thus starting her real estate business.

Hou Hailiang can also be considered a risk seeker in that he was willing to incur a high level of debt. Unlike other enterprises in the book, Original Enterprise has had a high debt ratio over the course of its development. Hou borrowed several hundred thousand RMB from relatives and friends when he founded the company. Then in 2002, Original Enterprise took out a bank loan of more than RMB 1 million. During the high-growth years of 2002 and 2003, Hou introduced another major shareholder who invested several million RMB, half of which was a loan. In 2003, Hou received a bank loan to buy a plot of land and then used the land as collateral to get another loan, part of which was used to build factories. Once the factories were fully operational, he was able to pay back the loans. His bank loans totaled about RMB 20 million.

Diligence and Hard Work

For the entrepreneurs who had started from scratch, being diligent and hardworking are probably the most important individual characteristics. As mentioned earlier, Aiminger's Liu Qiongying came from a poor rural family and began taking responsibility for household chores at an early age. She entered business in an attempt to rise above her poverty and bore physical hardships to build the business. Eitong Air Express's Lou Xiuhua showed similar determination. Because express services were unknown among most businesses when she and her husband launched the business, the two visited companies door-to-door to introduce their business.

The hard physical labor that Opple's Wang Yaohai suffered in his duck and fish farming days contributed to his determination to make a business from his "brainpower." The same could be said for Cao Xianglai. He took on various small jobs when he first arrived in Hainan before making his first break. Having faced financial and physical hardships, our entrepreneurs became better prepared for the difficulties and determined to start their own businesses.

Craving for Success, Never Surrender to Defeat

Those in business experience frequent setbacks and failures before finding success. This is the most challenging aspect for most entrepreneurs. Among our group of 20, the characteristic of never surrendering to defeat plays a central role in their sustainability.

Bridge HR's Hou Zhengyu admits that the breakup with his girlfriend at the time prompted him to seek his fortune in Shanghai. It was his poor family background and dim future prospects as a teacher that contributed to their breakup. Hou says there was only one thing on his mind: "I will never give up. I'll show her that I'm capable of earning a lot of money. Even if she gets married to someone else, I'll return wealthy enough to win her back."

Chang Xuehong of Compass Global Freight says he had been a rather timid boy until high school when he became involved in competitions between two groups of classmates. "By that time, I realized that I had to be strong, both in character and other aspects, otherwise I would be bullied by others," he says. Although his initial attempts at entrepreneurship did not go well, it was his strength of character and self-confidence that eventually led him to where he is now. "I've always had great faith in myself—I'll never be defeated by failure."

Many of the entrepreneurs we interviewed have steadfast perseverance and strong willpower. These qualities keep them moving forward despite difficulties and setbacks. Lou Xiuhua of Eitong Air Express represents an example in this area. To cut costs in the early days of the operation, wages were not high and did not attract a "high quality" of personnel. One employee stole everything that could be taken from the office, including a bike and a beeper, which was very expensive at that time. "Even the carton boxes used to hold things were taken. All that was left was the empty office," Lou says.

It would not be the last time something like this happened at the company. By 1997, Eitong had opened branches beyond Hangzhou. The manager of the Suzhou branch started his own company, taking all of Eitong's employees and customers. He copied the software the company had developed and sabotaged the remaining computers. Another time, another branch manager stole RMB 100,000 that he collected from customers. To make things worse, similar betrayals occurred in five branches within one month. "It was due to my steadfast endurance that I survived these setbacks and didn't give up," Lou says calmly. Of course, after these incidents, she began to formulate rules on the management of the company. She hired legal counsel and signed "covenants not to compete" with her managers.

Liang Qihua of KeyPoint Controls also suffered many setbacks in his business. He quit his job at the Shanghai Aerospace Bureau in 1996 and borrowed RMB 100,000 from friends and classmates, spending RMB 10,000 purchasing a distressed company. His business line was telephone exchanges and computer voice recognition systems, but the company lasted only four months. He then went to Shenzhen, but was unable to find work, so he returned to his hometown in Wuhan briefly. A classmate approached him to be the agent for an American instruments and meters company, and he gradually became a sales manager. But he left the company due to conflict with his boss. In 2000, Liang started a joint venture with three others, but it ended due to a lack of common goals. In spite of all the ups and downs, it was Liang's steadfast perseverance and strong willpower that sustained him through all the difficulties.

Hou Hailiang of Original Enterprise is also a person who does not give up easily. Many people start businesses just to make money, but Hou is an entrepreneur in the real sense of the word—he is dedicated to the ideal of building a long-term, sustainable enterprise. However, he also realizes the limitations of his management capabilities and the lack of resources. "A very important thing for an entrepreneur is that he or she must have faith in perseverance. When I was experiencing a particularly hard time, I always told myself, 'Hold on. Don't give up.'"

Credibility and Brotherhood

Among those we interviewed, quite a few believe that credibility and brotherhood played an important role. This is especially the case with customer relations. Tony Zhang says, "A general belief is that no businessman is credible. I'm not really that kind of businessman. I'm very sincere and honest with my customers. If a problem arises, I will do anything to guarantee their interests." Many of Tony's customers today have been with him for more than 10 years. They remain customers even if other companies offer lower prices. In building loyalty, Tony maintains that what is more important than good-product quality, good service, and stable supply is credibility. "Even in times of extremely tight supply and the consequent market price hikes, we'll stick to our promised price," he says.

Cao Xianglai of Zhongxin Chemical treats his customers as friends and brothers. As a result, a relationship of brotherhood has been forged and they help each other in times of difficulty. During his work with the state-owned CNCCC, he offered help to many customers. For instance, when a customer faced cash flow problems, Cao gave him advance payment to help him pull through. These customers became Cao's friends. When Cao started his own business, they offered much help, including support with cash flow.

In the eyes of Lu Wenlong of Hightex, credibility is essential to the establishment of an effective corporate culture. Credibility should start with the boss, Lu says: "Never put yourself as a mercenary businessman in the mind of your employees. Otherwise, it'll be hard to build up the corporate culture. You must let them realize that you are working with them toward a common goal. Only in this way can you build a cohesive team." Credibility should also be observed by the employees. Lu often told his employees: "Credibility is of great importance to an enterprise. But its importance to an individual is greater. You could leave Hightex. But without personal credibility, how could you expect other companies to accept you?" Lu thought that the combination of the credibility of the boss with the credibility of the employees could nurture an environment conducive to the build-up of an effective corporate culture.

Cultivating and Effectively Using Guanxi

Guanxi (people network) plays an especially important role in Chinese society, especially in economic activities. There are no well-established individual and enterprise credit systems in China, which means before you decide on reaching a business deal with an individual or enterprise, there is no sufficient track record of the relevant party's credit history for your reference. In China, rules and regulations often leave much room for flexibility. Depending on different circumstances, the same regulation can have different interpretations and implementing requirements. All these make rules and regulations in China less reliable. Instead, the Chinese tend to rely more on *guanxi*, because it is more reliable. *Guanxi* is essentially an unofficial bond of mutual responsibility and requires mutual trust, mutual loyalty, and mutual benefit. It is a key resource for Chinese businessmen. Some of the entrepreneurs we interviewed admit that the ability to cultivate and effectively use *guanxi* has also been important to their success.

Liang Qihua of KeyPoint Controls says he put great emphasis on the build-up of his people network. After a certain period of contact, both his customers and suppliers would take him as a trustworthy friend and consider KeyPoint as a good business partner. "Some customers didn't have dealings with us for three to four years. But when I went to them, they treated me like an old friend," Liang says. So how does one build and maintain this kind of *guanxi*? Liang says he showed kindness to others, not for business advantages but instead out of sincerity. In this way, many close and authentic friendships were formed.

Lu Wenlong of Hightex emphasized two points out of his personal experience on building up a network: first, you must be sincere; second, you should be generous with money. He says he read *Bel-Ami* by Maupassant when he was still a young boy. The story was about how the hero made his way from the bottom of the social ladder to the upper class. The story left a deep impression in him and he learnt much from it. When he worked as a clerk for a TVE, he sometimes spent his entire month's wage building *guanxi*. Later when the director of the TVE could not get a bank loan, Lu helped him get one through his *guanxi*.

In the early 1990s, the flow of market information in China was undeveloped. Businesses, especially foreign companies, had little idea about the market. One way to obtain vital information was through *guanxi*, a method used by Tony Zhang. "Information is very important in the trading business," Tony says. "If you have an extensive people network, you can gain lots of information through unofficial channels before it is public. If properly used, information gained through these channels can net huge profit." We have already described a transaction whereby Tony used *guanxi* information to profit from the purchase of doxycline, which he bought at RMB 200,000 per ton and sold at RMB 1.5 million per ton.

It is obvious that certain individual characteristics are essential to the success of the entrepreneurs we interviewed. These include a very strong willpower, an ambition to change the status quo, and the courage of not surrendering to defeat. In addition, they paid much attention to building up a people network and held credibility in high esteem.

10

Compete with Them

China's huge population makes it a great marketplace both in terms of the low-cost labor force and the consumer base. When this is combined with the continued economic growth in recent years, China has become a crucial market in international businesses' global competition strategies. According to *Sun Tzu on the Art of War,* the most well known ancient Chinese classical war book, "if you know the enemy and know yourself, you need not fear the result of a hundred battles." For foreign enterprises in China, knowing the strengths and weaknesses of domestic Chinese enterprises—especially private enterprises that contribute half of China's GDP—is the process of "knowing the enemy." In this chapter, we will analyze the strengths and weaknesses of Chinese POEs through an interpretation of the management style of the entrepreneurs we interviewed. Through the competition stories between the three local Chinese big POEs and their rivaling MNCs in the China market at the beginning of the book, we've gained a certain understanding on the local POE rivals MNCs face: the local POEs' grasp and knowledge of the China market and the Chinese customers is hard to replicate by the MNCs. Their interpretation of the market and their intuitive decision-making are also quite different from MNCs' data-based decision-making process. They have the courage to challenge against and compete with the formidable MNC rivals. They know how to use the strategy of "starting from countryside, then penetrating into cities" in China and are content with starting from the low-end market. They are very good at detecting and filling a market vacancy. What's more important, they keep moving up the value chain in their growth.

Strengths of Chinese Startup POEs

The strengths of Chinese startup POEs include:

- Insight into the market dynamics and opportunities in China
- Familiarity with the operational mechanism of government and making use of it
- Flexibility and quick response resulting from the individual decision-making
- Efficiency

Insight into the Market Dynamics and Opportunities in China

Insight into the market dynamics and opportunities is based on one's familiarity with the market and keen business sense. It is especially important when an enterprise enters new business areas or launches new products. Many of our 20 entrepreneurs possess this insight.

When Liu Qiongying of Aiminger Leather Goods began selling gym shoes at the end of the 1980s, the standard of living was rather low. However, demand for more expensive and fashionable goods was emerging. Given that the average monthly wage was only about several dozen RMB, Liu's gym shoes and leather shoes at over RMB 100 were virtually a luxury for most Chinese consumers. The fact that her shoes sold well was a reflection of this emerging market.

Lou Xiuhua showed insight when she identified the movement of businesses from Taiwan and Hong Kong into southern China. She realized that the influx of companies would also mean the increased demand for not only mail service between Hong Kong and the Pearl River Delta area, but more specifically express mail service for documents and product samples, leading to the establishment of Eitong Air Express.

Watching the market, Lou also saw the growing development in eastern China and recognized the value of setting up in Hangzhou, where there were no competitors and a growing number of businesses setting up in the region. Within its first year, Eitong Air Express earned RMB 200,000 a month. In the first few years of operation, the gross profit margin reached 100% to 200%.

It was while Hou Zhengyu of Bridge HR was working at the Hudong Shipbuilding Company as a safety inspector that he observed two key factors that led to his success. Many laborers were coming from rural areas to Shanghai to find work. This corresponded with the growing number of foreign companies that required a large number of laborers. "Where and how are these laborers recruited?" Hou asked himself. "It would be a great idea if the demand from foreign companies could be met with the surplus of rural workers."

The above examples are about entrepreneurs who started up their businesses after finding a business opportunity through some market insight. As for Han Yan of Wangu Textile, it was a matter of switching to a new industry after detecting a good opportunity. Armed with the expertise he gained in software development for textile manufacturers, he noticed that China's silk industry was at a low ebb, providing a very good entry point.

Familiarity with the Operational Mechanism of Government and Making Use of It

As mentioned in previous chapters, some of the featured entrepreneurs have worked with SOEs or government agencies. They became familiar with the workings of government agencies and took advantage of this knowledge both in selecting their business area and in procuring profitable projects.

During Tony's Group's transformation from a single-business line to a multi-business line, Tony Zhang obtained an important piece of information: the Shanghai municipal government was inviting public bidding for an agricultural project in Nanhui, a suburban district. Ten days before the bidding, Tony sought help from a CEIBS alumnus who recommended that he contact a professor as well as a senior engineer from the Shanghai Municipal Gardening Bureau. Tony hired the two experts to design a proposal based on his idea for a tourism-based agricultural project. The proposal won the bidding by a large margin among all the competing proposals. One of the main reasons why Tony was so determined to get this project was that it was a municipal government–sponsored project for guaranteeing the vegetable supply to Shanghai residents. There were various favorable government policies and subsidies for this project.

Bridge HR's business is all about supplying labor, which requires frequent contact with various government agencies. Hou had good standing with the government, he was a member of the local political consultative conference, he was selected as a national model young entrepreneur by the Central Committee of the Communist Youth League, and State Vice Premier Hui Liangyu had given a written approval for him and his business model. These served as very effective "political cards" whenever he had difficulties in dealings with related government agencies.

Hou also obtained the help of local governments when he wanted to establish cooperative deals with 50 technical schools to maintain the supply of trained and skilled laborers. He also co-invested with the local government to establish two national key technical schools. In the mid-1990s, Hou's hometown launched a campaign to promote the export of labor to cities as a means to generate income. They offered subsidies to companies that placed residents as well as for those who offered them training.

Tong Liqun of Runway Technology used his thorough understanding of the subtle interpersonal relations within government agencies to win business projects. Around the end of 1996, China planned to introduce from America the most advanced frame relay and APN (Access Point Name) technology in the world at that time. Both the banking sector and the Directorate General of Telecommunications (DGT) of China intended to establish their nationwide frame relay and APN backbone networks through public bidding. To build the backbone network of the banking sector and the data bureau, the DGT jointly set up a company to invite bidding on construction of the banking sector's network, while the DGT itself was in charge of the invitation for bidding and construction of its own network. The two American companies that took part in the bidding were CISCO and Sycamore Networks (which was later acquired by Ascend). CISCO won the first bid despite the fact that its quote was 50% higher than that of Sycamore. CISCO had been a long-time partner with the banking sector. There was very good mutual trust between the two.

While many companies competed to be the agent for Sycamore, Runway Technology was no longer considered a serious candidate. After all, among the competitors for Sycamore's agent business, Datang Telecom Technology and AsiaInfo Holdings were on the list of top 10 integrators of China. However, when the bidding result for the banking sector was announced, almost all of the companies vying to be Sycamore's agent withdrew. It was generally believed that CISCO would win the bidding instead. At this time, Tong Liqun went to meet the person in charge of Sycamore's China business, telling him that Runway Technology could help them win the project. Without much hope for success, Sycamore prepared five sets of bidding documents according to Tong's proposal. Tong managed through his "channels" at the DGT to make sure that the documents reached the five top officials who were in charge of the bidding. Twenty days later, the bidding result for the DGT network was announced: Sycamore won. The result was a surprise to all industry insiders. Runway Technology won widespread recognition overnight.

"I know perfectly well how things are done there," Tong says of his success. There were two key figures involved in this issue. One was the chief of the Directorate General's data bureau that had established a joint venture with the banking sector. The other was the deputy director-general of the DGT for data business. The two shared similar ranking within the DGT, but differed sharply on a lot of issues. "Especially at the initial stage of domestic digital businesses, it's hard to judge who has the right approach. So, both of their views seemed to have reasonable grounds in their own right," Tong says. But as a result of this disagreement, the two senior officials always took opposite approaches to finding solutions to problems. If one chose to move eastward, the other would move westward. Consequently, as the data bureau and the banking sector had chosen CISCO, the DGT would choose Sycamore. That was a fact Tong knew with certainty.

The Flexibility and Quick Response Resulted from the Individual Decision-Making

Almost every entrepreneur interviewed adopted individual decision-making in the management of their enterprises, although they also held discussions with their management team to listen to different opinions.

According to Cao Xianglai of Zhongxin Chemical, decision-making was a process from "democracy" to "centralism." On major issues concerning corporate strategy or development, Cao would first listen to the opinions of his management team, which were formulated into a draft proposal. Cao would then make the decision based on the draft proposal. Tony Zhang of Tony's Group also says that he made decisions on his own. After thoroughly considering his decisions, he would present them to his management team and convince them to accept and implement them.

The same individual decision-making by the boss was also adopted by Bridge HR. But unlike Tony's method of implementation followed by convincing, Hou would demand his managers implement the decisions unless they could otherwise convince him. "Generally speaking, I'm very confident about the decisions I make," Hou says. "Once something is decided, it must be implemented right away." It is this rapid implementation of the decisions made that gives these private enterprises the flexibility and speed to respond to market conditions.

One extreme example of individual decision-making is Yan Han from Wangu Textile. "Once I've decided on a certain issue, whether managers approve or not, I'll insist that they carry them out first," Yan says. He and his management team hold weekly meetings to discuss the problems the company faces, including those on implementing Yan's decisions. "If I find their opinions reasonable, I'll let them do it in the correct way."

Efficiency

In addition to being the sole decision-maker, most of these entrepreneurs are general managers of their operations. Other than maximization of profits, another priority these companies all strive for is a high degree of efficiency. The best example of this is Merryland Real Estate. According to the local administrative regulations, real estate developers need to be certified in four main areas, ranging from land use to the starting of construction before the launch of a real estate project and the application for a certificate of advance sale. To get all the required certificates and approvals, a real estate developer needs application approval from over 60 government agencies. The whole process usually takes at least half a year and sometimes as much as 10 months. Merryland was able to accomplish this in three to four months.

Weaknesses of Chinese Startup POEs

The weaknesses of Chinese startup POEs include:

- The lack of a mature management team and standard processes
- Low entry barrier, and potential high competition from newcomers
- Reliance on a few big customers

The Lack of a Mature Management Team and Standard Processes

As we have mentioned, the entrepreneurs we interviewed all consider the lack of talented people a bottleneck in their development. The three stages of private Chinese enterprises from trader to manufacturer and from manufacturer to technology developer determine that sales are the first priority in the initial stage. Most human resources are focused on the development of the market and customers. The entrepreneurs could hardly spare time on team building, although many later hired professional managers. In the meantime, as the organization structure was small at the early stage, the absence of standard management processes made it easy to achieve high efficiency. Consequently, even with the continuous growth of the enterprises, very few of the entrepreneurs cared about establishing standard management processes. Zhongxin Chemical was an exception. As early as 2001 (the third year of its establishment), Zhongxin developed an ERP system to trace and control the whole operational process.

Low Entry Barrier, and Potential High Competition from Newcomers

The fact that all the entrepreneurs we interviewed started from scratch determined that they had to enter businesses that have low entry barriers for both capital and technology. But these low-entry businesses attract many other newcomers. One example is agenting for other companies' products (especially foreign companies). Nearly half of the enterprises we spoke with were agents. In the past decade, the profit margins of this type of business have continued shrinking because of increasing competition. Take Zhongxin Chemical for example: between 1995 and 2006, its trade volume increased by several dozen times, while its profit margin was reduced by 50%. To survive fierce competition, many enterprises have to transform their business models, or begin plans to improve their core competence.

Reliance on a Few Big Customers

Generally speaking, private Chinese enterprises have not reached a mature stage. The reliance on a few big customers is common among many of them today. Dynaforge Tools & Hardware is one such example. In 1999, Dynaforge started to market small hardware and tools under its own brand name and reached a deal with B&Q allowing its products to be sold in the British-owned DIY chain. In the last few years, 60% of Dynaforge's brand name products were sold in B&Q. In 2005, however, B&Q bought OBI, which had an exclusive agreement with a competitor of Dynaforge, so B&Q had to quit its cooperation with Dynaforge.

11

Collaborate with Them

In competitive collaboration, collaboration is used as a means to win over competition. Collaborative competition is the most effective way of competing. According to a report by Booz Allen Hamilton consulting firm, among over 2,000 corporate alliances they surveyed, 50% were made with former competitors. It is valuable for foreign companies entering the Chinese market to be aware of the potential opportunities in collaborating with private Chinese enterprises, as well as the potential pitfalls.

Possible Collaborative Opportunities with Chinese POEs

The possible collaborative opportunities with Chinese POEs include:

- Borrowing their local resources and know-how
- Outsourcing part of the business to them
- Collaborating with them in marketing and sales
- Collaborating with them in product design
- Upstream or downstream partners
- Investment or acquisition

Borrowing Their Local Resources and Know-How

Although authorities have liberalized and opened up the Chinese markets according to commitments upon WTO accession, there remain sectors that are restricted for foreign investors. Some sectors require foreign involvement be in the form of joint ventures with local partners, while ownership caps are placed in other industries. In the cases where a total ban remains, foreign companies can enter a collaboration with Chinese enterprises for the use of their resources and know-how.

One such example is in the employment services industry. According to current regulations, foreign ownership is limited to joint ventures in which they can own a maximum of 49%. SOE giants engaged in this business, such as FESCO and CIIC, are focused on the high-end lucrative markets of white-collar professionals and high-level executives. Prior to Bridge HR's entry in the market, there were no big players in the low-end blue- and grey-collar labor market, giving the company a head start in this area of business. Because labor placement services requires a degree of government dealings, Bridge HR is an attractive potential partner for foreign companies wishing to enter this market.

In March 2007, Merryland Real Estate and Hong Kong–based Cheung Kong Holdings set up a joint venture to develop a lakeside plot on Jinji Lake, a plot that Merryland and another real estate developer won in public bidding a year earlier. Across the lake is the Suzhou Industrial Park, an industrial and commercial project jointly developed by Singapore and Suzhou governments. Millions of dollars have been invested in its development and surrounding infrastructure and facilities, such as the Suzhou Logistics Center, the Technology Culture and Art Center, the International Exhibition Center, Zuoan Commercial Street, and Jinji Lake Commercial Plaza.

As a local real estate developer, Merryland was aware of the latest municipal development plan and policies concerning the Industrial Park. This greatly helps Merryland's selection of projects. Although the commercial real estate was still at the initial stage, the plot Merryland obtained is in a very good location, which naturally made it a target for giants such as Cheung Kong Holding.

Outsourcing Part of the Business to Them

China has become the world's manufacturing center. Outsourcing production to Chinese manufacturers is no longer a novelty. In fact, many foreign enterprises are outsourcing parts of their operations to Chinese companies so they can focus on key business areas.

Compass Global Freight is an example. Its main business was as an international freight agency, but it also provided domestic express delivery service once the cargo reached China's shores. This domestic service was included only as a value-added service for the company's key international clients. Compass treated this portion of the business as an outsourcing service. It stationed its employees in the customers' factories to better meet their special demands. The on-site service helped reduce the customer's overhead costs and improve efficiency and reliability of the domestic express delivery service. It also strengthened the customer relationship.

Collaborating with Them in Marketing and Sales

In October 2004, China's second largest market player in shoe-making, Aokang, announced the establishment of cooperative partnership with the 300-year-old Italian shoemaker Geox. As the only cooperative partner of Geox in the world, Aokang Group and the Italian shoemaking giant will cooperate in the design, development, production, and sales of leather shoes around the world. In addition to being the OEM of Geox, Aokang will be involved in the development and design of Geox's products targeted for the Asian market. Aokang will also take charge of Geox's brand promotion, network building, and product sales in China. On the other hand, Geox will allow Aokang to use its global sales network to sell Aokang products, and Geox agrees to give Aokang brand first priority on its list of recommended products. As a matter of fact, by the time of this partnership deal, Geox had already moved its Asian research and development center from Hong Kong to Dongguan of south China's Guangdong Province.

Aokang is a private-owned enterprise in Wenzhou set up in 1988. It has grown into a well-known Chinese shoemaker with total assets of more than RMB 1 billion, three major production bases, and over 30 world-class production lines, turning out more than 10 million pairs of shoes annually. Aokang has over 2,000 brand shops and 800 shops in big department stores and shopping malls. It has opened branches in Italy, Spain, the US, and Japan. Three shoe design centers in Wenzhou, Guangzhou, and Milan develop over 3,000 new product designs annually.

Aokang's exclusive agent contract with Geox will end in August 2008. So far, Aokang has set up nearly 300 Geox brand shops in

China's first-tier cities. Aokang will continue to be Geox's biggest global OEM. In addition, Aokang's annual production for Geox will increase from the current 1 million to 4 to 5 million in the future.

In January 2008, Aokang signed a global strategic cooperation agreement with the famous Italian brand Valleverde, and purchased Valleverde's brand usage and operation in terms of sales and distribution worldwide for 10 years. According to the agreement, Aokang acquired the exclusive right of Valleverde's brand operation and production. Valleverde simply transformed into an "R&D department" offering support in terms of R&D resources and legal issues, and helping Aokang set up an international R&D center in Italy. The first Valleverde fleet shop operated by Aokang has opened in Shanghai's best downtown commercial street. Aokang plans to open at least 130 Valleverde brand shops in China's first-tier cities and penetrate into seven new markets, including the US, Japan, Russia, Thailand, and Singapore.

Collaborating with Them in Product Design

Established in 1986, Geely Group started with producing refrigerator parts. It entered the auto industry in 1997 and produced the first Geely automobile in 1999. Now Geely has been ranked as one of the top 10 auto producers of China. For a Chinese auto maker such as Geely, its strength lies in the low local production cost and the widespread sales channels, while its weakness is in auto design. Geely's rapid growth is attributed to its collaboration with foreign auto makers and auto project companies in design.

In December 2002, Geely reached a strategic cooperative deal with Auto Projects Group of Italy. The deal is mainly about the design of a series of family cars. Auto Projects Group is well known in auto shape engineering design, auto prototype making, and mould development and making. Its customers include famous car makers such as Ferrari and Mercedes-Benz. It is one of the leading companies in mould making and auto engineering design in Europe. In the same month, Geely signed technological cooperation deals with five companies, including Daewoo. The five companies would help Geely design the new models to be launched in 2004. Half a year later in June 2003, Geely signed another technological cooperation deal with the German Rucker AG, according to which Rucker would design an economic family car for Geely.

Geely's deal with Auto Projects Group of Italy is a kind of purchase—purchasing the models designed by the latter. The deal with Daewoo and the other four companies is to acquire the latter's assistance in design and development. The deal with the German Rucker AG is a kind of outsourcing—outsourcing the design to Rucker and asking Rucker to design a model according to Geely's requirements.

In October 2006, Geely and the British MBH announced a joint venture deal, with Geely holding a 51% share, Maple (a subsidiary of Geely) holding a 1% share, and MBH holding 48%. MBH is the producer of the famous black taxi cab TX4. The joint venture will produce the TX4 in China. This will significantly reduce the production cost of the TX4. One senior executive of MBH said: "Geely has a well-functioning sales network in China. The cooperation with Geely will offer MBH access to the whole China market, while Geely will acquire through the deal the advanced technology and IPR of our famous brand."

Upstream or Downstream Partners

Building alliances with suppliers or customers can bring about many benefits. Common goals and interests, together with the synergy created by industry/supply chain integration, will help generate more added value. Chinese POEs realize the importance of downstream and upstream cooperation, making it possible for cooperative opportunities with them. Take KeyPoint Controls as an example. After two failed joint ventures, KeyPoint introduced two investors: one a supplier, the other a customer. Another example is the producer and seller of cable materials, Original Enterprise. The company was seeking cooperative opportunities along the industry chain, and one of the potential partners was a cable producer. If they could reach a cooperative deal, Original would move a step downstream and turn from a cable material producer into a cable producer.

Bridge HR has focused on supplying blue- and grey-collar workers to foreign manufacturing enterprises based in Shanghai. So far, the company has more than 90% of this market. In addition, Bridge has its own technical schools that guarantee the supply of competent workers. This has given Bridge a competitive advantage over its competitors who use a low-price strategy. Bridge also hosts regular forums through its HR club that features industry experts speaking to HR decision-makers. In this way, Bridge has built up its name among its target customer group, and has become a long-term partner with big foreign companies such as Samsung and Ricoh.

Investment or Acquisition

As mentioned earlier, obtaining financing has been a major difficulty for most private Chinese enterprises. It has even become a factor preventing them from further development. Because further difficulties lie ahead, some companies may be willing to accept foreign investment or be acquired by bigger companies. Original Enterprise is one such example. It set up a joint venture with Italian-based Padanaplast, but there have been some conflicts in terms of strategy, and pressure is coming from both upstream customers and downstream suppliers, causing Hou Hailiang to rethink the joint venture: "In the past, when I couldn't reach consensus with partners I would try my best to repurchase his shares and carry out things my way. Now, so long as it is conducive to the healthy development of the company and the continuous growth of our business, I can temporarily make concessions."

Lu Wenlong of Hangzhou Hightex is planning a new business model that consists of opening a shopping center for household products. The center will feature dozens of showrooms featuring different rooms of a home, such as living rooms, bedrooms, and kitchens. Customers can get ideas on how to use and display products on sale, much like how IKEA operates. But unlike other similar outlets, this will feature the work of top designers, which will greatly add to the quality and interest levels. In addition, the center will combine different categories and group them with different lines of products. Lu says that if he does not have sufficient funds to implement this business model, he would like to introduce it to investors or partners.

Potential Caveats of Cooperating with Chinese POEs

Potential threats of cooperating with Chinese POEs include:

- Are they in an attractive industry?
- Are they willing to accept any form of partnership?

Are They in an Attractive Industry?

At the very beginning of *Competitive Advantage*, Michael Porter wrote: "Two central questions underlie the choice of competitive strategy. The first is the attractiveness of industries for long-term profitability and the factors that determine it." From this, we can see the importance of industry attractiveness to enterprise profitability.

Many Chinese POEs that have started from scratch are in industries with very low entrance barriers. This exposes them to the threat of new entrants. In the face of increasingly fierce competition, many industry players adopted a low-cost strategy. An example of this is the express delivery industry. To secure more market share, many competitors charged only RMB 5 for their express delivery service within Jiangsu, Zhejiang, and Shanghai. In such a cutthroat environment, express delivery companies had to reduce labor costs or adopt franchising operations. (To minimize cost, the franchiser neither provided any training to nor had any involvement in the management of the franchisees. The only connection between them was profit sharing.) This resulted in a general low quality of employees engaged in this business. There were frequent losses of goods, and late delivery was even more prevalent. Within an express delivery company, it was not uncommon for front line employees or managers to disappear with company assets and customers' payments.

In some industries, suppliers have very strong bargaining power and are able to squeeze the profits of enterprises. Original Enterprise was in such an industry. Its business lines were the production and sale of cable materials. The price of its main raw materials—copper and petrol-chemical products—rose sharply in recent years. And it is very difficult for Original Enterprise to transfer the increased cost to its downstream customers. So its profits have continued shrinking for the past few years. Hou Hailiang had to give up the concept of absolute control over the enterprise's future development. Now he is willing to accept an acquisition deal.

In some other industries, buyers have very strong bargaining power. The *guanxi* with buyers is a major means of securing more market share. An example of this is the telecommunications engineering industry in which Zhicheng Communication operates. The General Manager of Zhicheng, Cui Lijian, started without any industry background. To build up *guanxi*, he spent much effort to become friends with influential people in the industry. His unique way of building up and maintaining *guanxi* lowered the economic cost. In addition, *guanxi* built up this way is usually more stable than those bought by money.

Are They Willing to Accept Any Form of Partnership?

Instinctively, Chinese private entrepreneurs do not like the idea of joint venture or any partnership that may limit their decision-making. However, with the growth of their enterprises, they have come to realize the limitations of their resources. And for the sake of growth, a number of entrepreneurs have begun to accept joint ventures or alliances, but many of them still hope to retain control of the enterprise.

As we mentioned under the "collaborative opportunities" heading, Bridge HR is a very promising candidate for collaboration. However, the general manager has a strong sense of control over the company. Hou Zhengyu says he must retain a controlling share either in introducing investors or in forming a joint venture. "Even in our contacts with venture capital investors, we insist on holding at least 80% of the enterprise shares."

Opple is also a good candidate for foreign investors, but Opple's General Manager, Wang Yaohai, is cautious about the introduction of external capital. He says: "Capital is a really good thing when you need it. But once it is introduced into the company, you also have to handle some difficult situations." He is even cautious on the issue of going public: "Before going public, you need to figure out the purpose for doing so. So far, I haven't figured it out yet."

Several years ago when there were not so many joint ventures or public companies in China, there might have been many Chinese private enterprises that would have been willing to form joint ventures or alliances with foreign companies. Many of them would have chosen to go public (including on the overseas stock market). However, after witnessing so many internal integration problems among the parties of joint ventures, as well as the strengthened domestic and overseas regulations on the public companies, Chinese private entrepreneurs have realized that capital is a double-edged sword. As long as they have other means to obtain capital, they will not likely choose a joint venture, alliance, or going public. In a sense, is this not a reflection of their experience, maturity, and wisdom?

APPENDIX A

Interview Questions

Please give a brief introduction of your personal background and experience growing up.

Please give a brief introduction about your experience setting up your enterprise and its current status.

Please give a brief introduction of the industry your enterprise is engaged in.

What is your perspective of the industry? Are you planning to enter other industries or areas, or will you continue to focus on the present industry?

Which type of enterprise is your main competitor (POEs, SOEs, or FIEs[1])?

Where does the competitive advantage of your enterprise lie? Is it in strategy, business model, or marketing?

What stages of growth has your enterprise gone through? What are the corresponding strategies and priorities in management for the different stages?

What is your present strategy? What is the biggest challenge in implementing the strategy?

What is the organizational structure of your enterprise? How does it evolve into the status quo?

What measures have you taken in areas of corporate culture, recruitment, employee training, and incentive mechanism?

Do you think the capital structure of your enterprise is reasonable? What is your biggest problem in financing? How do you solve it?

What do you think are the bottlenecks in your future development?

Is your spouse, child/children, or other relatives involved in the management and operations of your enterprise?

What are the respective advantages and disadvantages in running the enterprise by "insiders" and running the enterprise by "professional managers"?

In your opinion, what personality characteristics are most important to success?

Note

1. There are three main forms of foreign investment in China: equity joint venture, the cooperative or contractual joint venture, and the wholly-foreign-owned enterprise. They are collectively called foreign investment enterprises (FIEs).

APPENDIX B

List of Companies

Company Name	Year of Establishment	Location of Headquarters	Place of Startup	Leader Name	Year of Birth	Sex	Native Province	Education	Industry
Aiminger Leather Goods Manufacturing Company of Chengdu	1995	Chengdu	Chengdu	Liu Qiongying	1970	Female	Sichuan	Junior Middle School	Manufacturing of Shoes
Bridge HR	2003	Shanghai	Shanghai	Hou Zhengyu	1969	Male	Jiangsu	Non-degree College	Employment Service
Dynaforge Tools & Hardware Co., Ltd.	1997	Shanghai	Shanghai	Jason Zhang	1969	Male	Shanghai	College	Foreign Trade (tools and hardware)
Eitong Air Express Co., Ltd.	1995	Shanghai	Hangzhou	Lou Xiuhua	1968	Female	Zhejiang	College	Express Delivery
Essence Technology Solution, Inc.	2003	Shanghai	Shanghai	Chen Xin	1969	Female	Shanghai	College	IC Design
Fortune Automobile Racing Club	2000	Shanghai	Wenzhou	Michael Ma	1965	Male	Zhejiang	Senior Middle School	Automobile Racing
Guangdong Opple Lighting Co., Ltd.	1995	Guangdong	Guangdong	Wang Yaohai	1967	Male	Zhejiang	Senior Middle School	Manufacturing of Lighting Products
Hainan Zhongxin Chemical Co., Ltd.	1997	Shanghai	Hainan	Cao Xianglai	1966	Male	Hubei	College	Trade (mainly foreign trade) of Chemicals
Hangzhou Wangu Textile Co., Ltd.	1997	Hangzhou	Hangzhou	Yan Han	1957	Male	Zhejiang	Non-degree College	Textile
Hightex Co., Ltd., Hangzhou	1999	Hangzhou	Hangzhou	Lu Wenlong	NA	Male	Zhejiang	Junior Middle School	Textile

Company			Leader					Industry
Name	Year of Establishment	Location of Headquarters	Place of Startup	Name	Year of Birth	Sex	Native Province	Education	
Runway Technology Co., Ltd.	1996	Beijing	Beijing	Tong Liqun	1966	Male	Beijing	College	Telecommunications Software
Shanghai Compass Global Freight Co., Ltd.	2003	Shanghai	Shanghai	Chang Xuehong	1967	Male	Hebei	College	International Cargo Freight Agency and Express Delivery
Shanghai KeyPoint Controls Co., Ltd.	2000	Shanghai	Shanghai	Liang Qihua	1967	Male	Hunan	Master Degree	Foreign Trade (agenting instruments and meters for petro-chemical industry)
Shanghai Original Enterprise Development Co., Ltd.	1997	Shanghai	Shanghai	Hou Hailiang	1963	Male	Henan	College	Manufacturing of Cable material
Shanghai Xhan Yang Chemical Co., Ltd.	2003	Shanghai	Shanghai	Cheryl Chen	1970	Male	Shandong	Non-degree College	Foreign Trade (chemicals: ink material)
SPN Technology Co., Ltd.	2000	Shanghai	Shanghai	Wang Zhi	1968	Male	Jilin	Master Degree	Foreign Trade (agenting automatic control systems for engineering machinery)

(Continued)

Company				Leader					Industry
Name	Year of Establishment	Location of Headquarters	Place of Startup	Name	Year of Birth	Sex	Native Province	Education	
Suzhou Merryland Real Estate Development Co., Ltd.	1997	Suzhou	Suzhou	Gao Qi	1967	Female	Jiangsu	Non-degree College	Real Estate
Tianjin Longtaixiang Metal Products Co., Ltd.	2000	Tianjin	Tianjin	Song Qiang	1969	Male	Tianjin	College	Import and Processing of Waste Metal
Tony's Group	1997	Shanghai	Shanghai	Tony Zhang	1962	Male	Sichuan	College	Foreign Trade (chemicals), Restaurant, Modern Agriculture and Real Estate
Zhicheng Communication	2002	Shanghai	Shanghai	Cui Lijian	1973	Male	Shandong	Non-degree College	Telecommunications Engineering

Bibliography

Blue Book of Non-State-Owned Economy 2005–2006. All-China Federation of Industry & Commerce.

Bai, Shouyi. *An Outline History of China.* Foreign Languages Press, 2002.

Cai, Fang, and Lin Yifu. *China's Economy.* China Financial & Economic Publishing House, 2003.

Dong, Fureng. *The Economic History of the People's Republic of China.* Economic Sience Press, 1999.

Editorial Board of Exploring Civilization Series. *Exploring Civilization—The Han Dynasty.* Daxiang Publishing House, 2002.

Huyghe, Francois-Bernard, and Edith Huyghe. *The Empire in the Mirage: People on the Silk Road, Deities and Mythology.* Kashgar Uighur Publishing House, 2004.

Lan, Yong. *A Historic Geography of China.* Higher Education Press, 2002.

Ma, Licheng. *The Great Breakthrough—The Evolution of Private Economy in China.* All-China Association of Industry and Commerce Publishing House, 2006.

Ning, Yi. *Chinese Business Wisdom: The Secret to Success of Shanxi, Anhui and Zhejiang Merchants.* Dizhen Publishing House, 2006.

Pan, Xiaoping. *Anhui Merchants: the No.1 Merchant Group of the Ming and the Qing Dynasties.* China Radio & Television Publishing House, 2005.

Porter, Michael. *Competitive Advantage.* Free Press, 1998.

Redding, S. Gordon. *The Spirit of Chinese Capitalism.* Walter de Gruyter Inc., 1995.

Ronan, Colin A. *The Shorter Science and Civilization in China.* Cambridge University Press, 1995.

Sun, Tao. *On Shanxi Merchants.* China Morden Economic Publishing House, 2006.

Wild, Oliver. *The Silk Road.* http://www.caissoas.com/CAIS/Geography/silk_road.htm, 1992.

Wu, Jinglian. *Understanding and Interpreting Chinese Economic Reform.* Yuandong: Publisher of Shanghai, 1999.

Wu, Xinhua. *The Ringing of Camel Bells: The Silk Road in Ancient China.* Chengdu: Sichuan People's Publishing House, 2004.

Xu, Dixin, and Wu Chengming. *A History of Chinese Capitalism: Chinese Capitalism in the New-Democratic Revolutionary Period.* People Press, 2005.

Xu, Dixin, and Wu Chengming. *A History of Chinese Capitalism: Chinese Capitalism in the Old-Democratic Revolutionary Period.* People Press, 2005.

Xu, Dixin, and Wu Chengming. *A History of Chinese Capitalism: the Emergence of Chinese Capitalism.* People Press, 2005.

Yun, Guanping, and Chen Qiaozhi. *Overseas Chinese Enterprises in South East Asia.* Economic Management Press, 2001.

Zhong, Pengrong. *The Code of Shanxi Merchants.* China Small Medium Enterprises, December, 2006.

Index